2018 | Issue #2

U.P. READER

Bringing Upper Michigan Literature to the World

A publication of the
Upper Peninsula Publishers and Authors Association (UPPAA)
Marquette, Michigan

MODERN
HISTORY
PRESS

U.P. Reader

Issue #1 is still available!

Michigan's Upper Peninsula is blessed with a treasure chest of writers and poets, all seeking to capture the diverse experiences of Yooper Life. Now U.P. Reader offers a rich collection of their voices that embraces the U.P.'s natural beauty and way of life, along with a few surprises.

The twenty-eight works in this first annual volume take readers on a U.P. Road Trip from the Mackinac Bridge to Menominee. Every page is rich with descriptions of the characters and culture that make the Upper Peninsula worth living in and writing about.

Available in paperback, hardcover, and eBook editions!

ISBN 978-1-61599-336-9

www.UPReader.org

SHORT STORIES
HUMOR
HISTORY
MEMOIR
POETRY
& MORE FROM *U.P.* WRITERS

BRINGING *UPPER MICHIGAN* LITERATURE TO THE WORLD

U.P. Reader: Bringing Upper Michigan Literature to the World -- Issue #2
Copyright © 2018 by Upper Peninsula Publishers and Authors Association (UPPAA). All Rights Reserved.

Learn more about the UPPAA at www.UPPAA.org

Cover Photo: "U.P. Wolf" by Mikel B. Classen. This was shot a few years back in northern Marquette County. That was back when I carried a Pentax and still shot with film. This was taken with a 200 mm telephoto lens on 35mm film. I've always felt that the wolf is the embodiment of the spirit of the Upper Peninsula. Loyal to its family, yet independent and tenacious, a creature that has overcome all odds to survive, the wolf's struggle reflects our struggles. There is no U.P. wilderness without the wolf. To hear the call of the wolf echoing across the untamed landscape is to truly live.

ISSN: 2572-0961

ISBN 978-1-61599-384-0 paperback
ISBN 978-1-61599-385-7 hardcover
ISBN 978-1-61599-386-4 eBook

Managing Editor - Mikel B. Classen
Associate Editor and Copy Editor - Deborah K. Frontiera
Production Editor - Victor Volkman
Cover Photo - Mikel B. Classen
Cover graphics and Layout - Michal Šplho, Design Amorandi

Distributed by Ingram (USA/CAN/AU), Bertram's Books (UK/EU)

Published by
Modern History Press
5145 Pontiac Trail
Ann Arbor, MI 48105

www.ModernHistoryPress.com
info@ModernHistoryPress.com

CONTENTS

Introduction

by Mikel B. Classen

Welcome to the second issue of the *U.P. Reader*. It is hard to believe that it has already been a year—and what a year it has been! When we started this adventure, like most, it was a journey into the unknown. And like most adventures, there's always the danger that everything could fall flat and die. Things could get ugly. Fortunately, that was not how this turned out. Bookstores liked it. Those that picked it up seemed to like it. Feedback was from favorable to excited. The *U.P. Reader* exceeded our expectations. We began working toward a Volume Two, but the first issue wasn't done surprising us.

The first issue of the *U.P. Reader* reached out and found its way to some surprising places. The state Library of Michigan requested that we submit the *U.P. Reader* to their Notable Books program. We did. We didn't win, but we were invited. Then we heard that two of the selections, Larry Buege's "Song of Minnehaha" and Frank Farwell's "Source" were both nominated for Pushcart's Best of the Small Press award. Results will be announced in late spring this year. So, that's still out there. Consequently, we were thrilled with the adventure of Volume One. If you missed the original Volume One, ask for it wherever you found Volume Two (which you are holding right now).

Now, I sit with the second issue in hand. I've seen the work and I realize how much improved Volume Two is. We have many of our favorite authors from the first issue, plus many new ones who are talented and fun. We have also included, for the first time, a "Young U.P. Authors" section. This evolved from the newly inaugurated Dandelion Cottage Short Story Contest (www. DandelionCottage.org) involving the Upper Peninsula public schools and put on by the Upper Peninsula Publishers & Authors Association (www.UPPAA.org). The entries were judged and the top two winners' stories appear in this issue. The *U.P. Reader* is proud to have these young writers aboard. It gives us a more rounded selection. I hope to continue this feature with every issue.

Volume Two has more writers and poets represented and more material, for which we doubled the size. It is my hope that, once again, the *U.P. Reader* will reach out and exceed not only our expectations, but also those set by Volume One. Onward to the next adventure!

If you have ever had the inclination to write poetry, prose, or stories, we invite you to join your neighbors in the UPPAA today.

Mikel B. Classen,
Managing Editor and
Deborah K. Frontiera,
Editor

Victor R. Volkman,
Production Editor

Tales from the Busy Bee Café

by John Argeropoulos

Yianni knew that the filming of the courtroom scenes for *Anatomy of a Murder* would continue for at least another hour or two, yet he was needed elsewhere. He had to reluctantly close his notebook and relinquish his coveted balcony seat in order to get back to the restaurant where his parents relied on him during the evening rush hour. The filming was a magnet for everyone in the area, including Yianni, but he knew that he would soon be involved with characters and stories every bit as interesting. He covered the five blocks to the Busy Bee Café quickly and was relieved to discover that he was not late for the main event.

Like clockwork, all the regulars began to assemble for what is best described as a form of gustatory street theater. Karl Manheim, a local DJ and a high-strung loner by nature, was the first to arrive. He sought out his usual stool at the far end of the counter near the door. It was a puzzling place to sit for a person who has just emerged from the confines of a hectic studio job since it was situated directly across from the small radio that was always blaring.

Karl had no sooner placed his favorite order for baked ham and picked up the local paper than he became visibly agitated and began shouting, "That damn Bolero!" Only a handful of people knew the inside joke that was being perpetrated by Bill Thompson, his colleague at WDMJ radio, who fiendishly selected all of Karl's most hated music for this time slot, knowing full well that Karl was a captive audience at the diner.

With uncanny timing, Ray Russo raced in, tossed his lunch bucket on the floor, and plopped down a couple stools away from Karl. In his characteristically obtuse manner, a mixture of natural ebullience and childlike innocence, Ray blurted out, "Is that *Madame Butterfly*?"

"Madame *Nhu*, you idiot!" scowled Karl.

The intended bullet missed its mark as Ray kept smiling blissfully, wondering aloud about how much things had changed since his Army days in Japan. The thought of it consumed him and Ray constantly talked of going back someday to find out. He had been saving every spare coin for that glorious day for the past three years, but he realized that it was just a dream and that it might never happen on the abysmally low wages he earned at the Cliffs Dow Chemical plant. He faithfully trekked the six mile roundtrip from his rooming house on Baraga Avenue every day, choosing to use the money saved on bus fares for his trip. Perhaps it was this motivation that propelled him with the speed that would be the envy of an Olympic race walker. "Race-Walker Ray" with the big smile and trusty lunch box was always a head turner on his way to work and back.

Lost in all the commotion was the "Bean Man," who had unobtrusively edged his way toward a view of the specials listed on the handwritten chalkboard that served as a menu. Barney's dress and demeanor never changed from visit to visit. A mousy-looking man with thick glasses, a floppy cap, and a long tattered coat to match his forlorn appearance, Barney's focus was riveted on the chalkboard. If he spotted his obsession for home-baked beans, a trace of a smile would briefly betray his great joy and he would quickly sit down. If the object of his delight was not included, he would turn, crestfallen at his misfortune, and slink out the door. On occasion he might muster the courage to ask about the beans, hoping against hope that they might have been somehow overlooked, but on this day he disappeared without a word.

Not at all amused by any of these proceedings, Oscar was holding court at the other end of the counter. A tall, brawny, bald man with a booming, resonant voice, he always wore a white flannel long-sleeve shirt and baggy black trousers with big red suspenders. Oscar bellowed about the fact that chemicals had ruined the taste of everything, including his favorite brand of beer, and that chemicals would soon be the death of us all.

Charlie, who was seated next to Oscar on the end stool next to the kitchen and who worked at the sawmill where Oscar was the night watchman, simply stared straight ahead and shook his head from time to time. He knew better than to challenge Oscar's ranting, but he also lacked the ability to speak beyond very simple statements about the weather or some other equally innocuous topic. Charlie would usually be the last customer to leave each night, often having spent hours drinking coffee and feeding the jukebox in an effort to forestall another lonely night at his shack on the south side of town. We all knew that he had been kicked out of school in the middle of the third grade for defying the school principal, Miss Macy, and that he never tried to return. His lot in life had been a series of low-paying, grueling jobs with little or no future, but he nonetheless exhibited a gentle quality and never whined about life's unfairness.

A group of workmen from a highway construction job began to file in from Joe's Tavern down the street. They always sat together at the same table and were a boisterous, fun-loving group of guys who liked their beer, good food, and tall tales as a way to banish their aches and pains. Most of the regulars tended to ignore them unless they happened to overhear a particularly funny story. Although they were usually loud, the workmen were mostly pretty well behaved and there was little reason for the regulars to interact with them. However, tonight there was an altercation that erupted so quickly and with such violence that everyone was stunned. It seems that one of them had a bit too much to drink and became engaged in a heated argument with a fellow at the next table, calling him a "jarhead." With lightning speed and a maniacal look in his eyes, the ex-Marine jumped to his feet, picked up a chair, and slammed it into the head of the offender. Blood was spurting all over the stricken man's face and shirt, some of it dripping down to the table and onto the floor.

What happened next caught most people by surprise. Everyone was bracing for some type of retaliation, but once it was determined that the wound was not life threatening, the group quickly decided to pay their bills and get out before any police showed up. Apparently this was not the first encounter between the two combatants and their friends were worried about possible jail time, which they hoped to avoid by taking their buddy to the emergency room and claiming that he had been injured on the job.

Tony, a local roofer who frequented the same bar, turned from his stool and laughed at the bedlam, saying that the jerk had it coming, and in fact was overdue for shooting his mouth off all the time. Nobody took issue with his comments and Tony resumed his meal, although he continued to mutter to himself about guys who couldn't hold their liquor.

The ensuing lull provided a respite in the kitchen where Sam, the owner-cook had been scurrying to keep up with the onslaught of orders. His wife, Angela, who labored as his faithful partner, took the opportunity to get some of the dishes washed and asked their son, Yianni, to keep an eye on the needs of the dining room. Being immigrants from Greece, the couple often unconsciously lapsed into their mother tongue, when they encountered a stressful situation like the fight.

Early Settler · Grand Island

Sam and Angela's comments were overheard by Max Geiger, who was seated at the back table nearest to the kitchen. Max did not take kindly to such talk, and he hollered, "Hey, talk American back there!"

Tony wheeled around on his stool and glared at Max. "You shut your mouth if you don't want some of what the last guy got."

Max's fiery temperament had served him well during his days as a hockey player who liked to mix it up and excite the crowds at the Palestra, but then a freakish accident suffered while working in a warehouse ruined everything. A pile of pallets collapsed and threw him against a row of large storage barrels, severely injuring his right hip and knee, permanently robbing him of his ability to continue his hockey career. Perhaps even worse, the incident also deprived him of a natural outlet to vent some of his aggressive personality and this left Max vulnerable at times like this when his temper got out of control.

Max started to get up, his hand wrapped tightly around his cane that could have served as a club, but he thought better of it. He realized that he would be no match for the bull-necked roofer, even though Tony was obviously showing the effects of his ritual round of boilermakers at Joe's.

Yianni glanced at his watch while refilling Charlie's bottomless cup, noting that it was already past 7 p.m. On most nights the dinner trade would be winding down about now, but this was Friday night. Friday night was *the* big night of the week because the downtown merchants stayed open until nine o'clock. Hordes of town folks would come streaming in from all directions, creating a shopping and entertainment frenzy.

Among the customers who only appeared on Friday nights was Pete Splake, who predictably ordered his usual hot pork sandwich with extra gravy. Sam had spotted him come in and had already started to prepare the order. Yianni could rarely get a word out of him, but he was fascinated by the stories that he had heard over the years. Splake had a reputation for being able to live off the land as a trapper, hunter, and fisherman of almost mythical proportions. Not only did he know where the best fishing was, but he could catch trophy-size fish by stealthily placing his hand in the water and actually stroking the belly of the fish before deftly snatching it out of the water. Yianni was lost in a deep reverie in which he imagined himself fishing alongside Pete Splake when he was quickly brought back to reality by Kayo's thundering greeting.

"Johnny, get your gun! Johnny, get your gun!"

Kayo was the gruff caretaker of the city dump and had taken to teasing Yianni about getting drafted if he didn't go to college next year. Kayo added to his meager pay by setting aside items like scrap iron, copper tubing, old tires that still had decent tread on them, and various pieces of broken furniture that he could repair. He was also a wicked pool player and was known to run the table on many unsuspecting young airmen from K.I. Sawyer who lost their hard-earned cash because they had mistakenly underestimated Kayo's skill based on his scruffy appearance. He really wasn't here for food right now as much as he was to learn the time and location of tonight's poker game. Unfortunately, Kayo's pool skills did not extend to poker, where he regularly lost most of the hustle money from his various enterprises, but he just couldn't resist coming back for more.

Kayo's teasing unwittingly turned out to be on the mark, but not in the way that Kayo had intended. Yianni wasn't worried about the draft at all, but about college, and whether he should even apply. In fact he often thought about enlisting in order to escape the conflict between his love for writing and the constant push by his high school teachers and principal to pursue a career in engineering. These well-meaning teachers were going on his stellar grades in science and math courses, but they failed to recognize that most of his success was due to fluency in Greek which, combined with four years of high school Latin, enabled Yianni to know most of the terminology without ever studying. His parents, of course, sided with the school because they feared that writing would not lead to any kind of job opportunity.

Sam and Angela were well aware of the notebook in which Yianni kept recording ideas for a proposed book, and they were troubled by his fierce determination to keep it as a private journal. It wasn't so much that they feared any kind of deep, dark secrets as much as the fact that it had become a barrier between them. They recognized that their son was bright and were quite proud of his achievements, but they also knew that he was very impressionable and tended to daydream. They worried that he was living in a fantasy world and that he was not developing an appreciation for how the real world worked.

Yianni would readily concede that he embellished the events he wrote about, but the journal served as his laboratory for trying to understand what makes people tick and how their lives had unfolded to this particular point. It helped him realize that each of us had many possible futures and provided glimpses of how his own life might evolve. Therefore, he would never believe that his writing represented a flight from reality or that he was out of touch with the real world.

To the contrary, Yianni knew intuitively that it would be a colossal mistake to become the prisoner of someone else's expectations, no matter how well intentioned and loving such advice might be. After months of agonizing about college, he was pleased that an exciting idea had emerged.

Yianni would submit a portion of his manuscript to a major magazine as a way of finding out if he should continue to entertain thoughts of a writing career, and if his short story was accepted, he could use it as leverage about what major to pursue. If not, he knew that engineering school would not be the right thing to do and Kayo's scenario would come true after all.

He could already hear the furor that would be unleashed by his parents if he were to enlist in the Army, but a new confidence now fueled his determination to hold his ground. Perhaps the fates would be kind and he might never have to cross that bridge. In any case, he was ready to roll the dice, certain that either course of action was better than remaining in limbo.

John Argeropoulos is an emeritus professor and former career counselor at Northern Michigan University, where he was employed for 31 years. John also coordinated the effort to establish the Northern Center for Lifelong Learning at NMU, a program that he and his wife (Mary) continue to enjoy in their retirement. Among many published articles, he has written on the history of the Greek community in Marquette County in *Harlow's Wooden Man* journal for the Marquette Regional History Center.

A Geology Geek Finds God

by Leslie Askwith

One Friday afternoon, the health department where I worked got a call from a woman on Drummond Island. Her family had rented a house for a reunion. She said everyone arrived feeling good and ready to relax by the river, but soon were moaning and running for the bathroom. People at the resort next door were getting sick too. Nausea, diarrhea, and vomiting were the miserable symptoms. She suspected it was their water.

I agreed with her. The island is known for its limestone, which is notorious to people in my line of work for cracks and fissures, open channels to the aquifer. A limestone ridge called the Niagara Escarpment juts from the earth in that part of the Upper Peninsula. It extends from Chicago to Niagara Falls and, not far west of the island, forms the largest cave system in Michigan near the village of Trout Lake.

I poured fluorescent dye into the toilet tank of the house, and the next day, dye flowed out of the house's taps. The septic tank had been installed directly on limestone bedrock and it leaked. Sewage was flowing through cracks in limestone to wells nearby.

I worked as an environmental health sanitarian at the Chippewa County Health Department, granting sewage and well permits, and it was my job to prevent contaminated sewage from reaching groundwater. Every spring when builders started clamoring for permits, I set out in my rusty Pathfinder, driving to isolated corners of the county to figure out if and where and

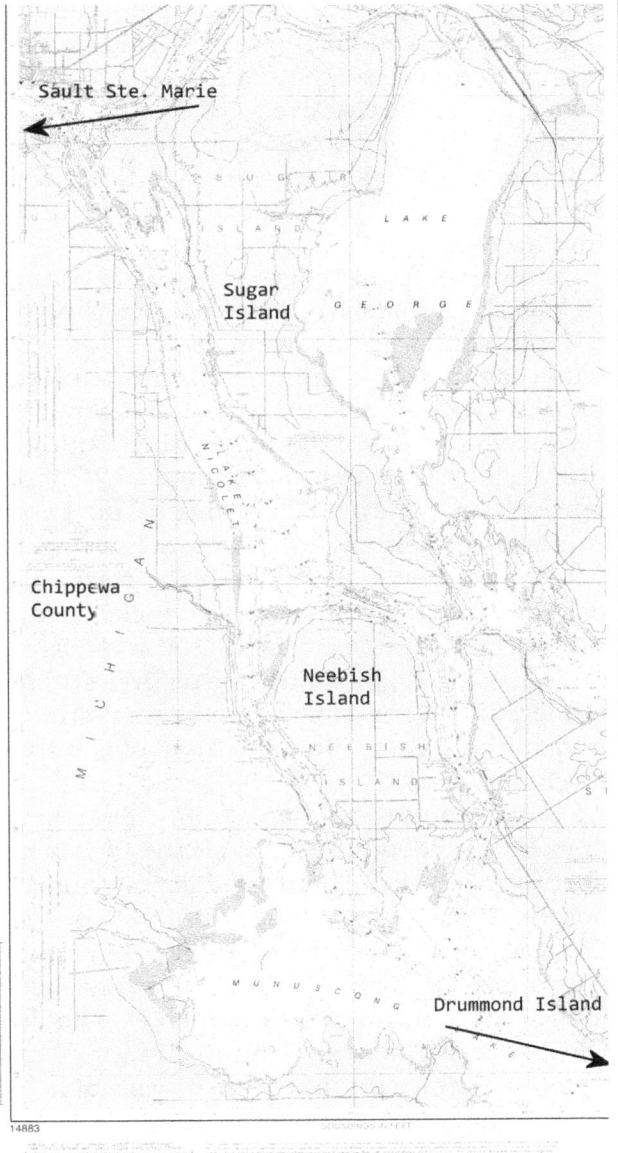

sewage disposal systems and wells could be installed. My work Bible was a hugely under-appreciated treasure trove of maps of the county's 63 types of soil—302 pages of aerial photos marked with squiggly lines delineate soils with names like Halfaday Sand, Beavertail Muck, and Rudyard Silty Clay Loam, which is different from Pickford Silty Clay Loam.

I LOVED my *Soil Survey of Chippewa County, Michigan*. It stripped the land of vegetation, revealing naked layers of glacial debris, muddy lake bottoms, and ancient coral reefs. I'd haul out my *Soil Survey* (it's thick and heavy enough to require hauling) to see what kind of soil would probably be there. A man who worked on the survey said he and others had walked the county with a hand auger, drilling holes every 50 feet or so until the entire county was mapped. Chippewa County is 1558 square miles of land, and even taking the possibility of exaggeration into account, that's a lot of holes.

I often met Cliff Tyner on Neebish Island. He'd lean on his shovel near me, chewing on a toothpick, wearing what looked like the same faded blue denim shirt with a bright blue X on the back under his suspenders. He'd spent a lot of backhoe time building drain fields for summer homes. "Schoolteachers from down below, puttin' up an A-frame shack," he said one time as I struggled with my auger to get through the rocky soil on Rue des Roches (Road of Rocks), slapping at mosquitoes. The St. Mary's River streamed past, glistening like a silver stream of mercury. Waterfront property was, still is, in demand. People liked the high lots on that stretch of road.

I dug through the glacial till, unearthing smooth rounded stones, evidence of having spent time in the glacial tumbler that moved across Chippewa county 10,000 years ago. Digging these holes throughout the county was a great geological puzzle, a geo-archeological dig. I was the first person ever to see these ancient stones. It didn't matter that none of them were likely to be valuable. It only mattered that I was the first to ever see them. Who knew what would be unearthed? There aren't many things that can be said

about that even in the sparsely populated eastern Upper Peninsula.

I was looking for a pocket of good soil deep enough to clean sewage before it got into the river or nearby wells. The regulations were specific...six feet of soil that's dry year-around, porous enough to let the water through, but not so full of open spaces that the soil particles can't do their work of wiping out viruses and bacteria. I pinched the dirt, felt for sandy grit, tested the clay content, watched for the stain of silt on my fingers and mottled stains in the soil indicating seasonal high water. Fortunately for the owner of the lot on Rue des Roches, the glacier had left behind suitable deposits.

Back at the dock I waited for the ferry, dangling my itchy feet in the river, sitting on a jagged boulder of limestone that had been blasted from the river to make the Rock Cut, a channel deep enough for ocean freighters. I picked up a bit of white limestone containing the imprint of a small mollusk that died 500 million years ago. It felt like a tiny grave in my hand. It was distressing to know the road commission ground that ancient graveyard into road gravel.

I realize this point of view mystifies most people, except for those who love the TV show, *The Big Bang Theory*, as I do, and who also think the writers are missing out by not including a geologist.

I had a favorite fossil on Drummond Island's Maxton Plains. Most common fossils are small bits of coral or shell, but this was a good-sized squid-like creature called Orthoceras. The plains are like a giant flat limestone parking lot, a cemetery for dead creatures that settled quietly to the bottom of the ocean that covered the area millions of years ago. Last time I looked for it, the Orthoceras was gone, probably chipped from its grave by someone. Cretin! They couldn't have gotten anything more than a bit of broken shards.

There's a slim chance I wasn't looking in the right place. But the plains draw a fair number of visitors and some people can't seem to let nature just be. The Nature Conservancy erected signs explaining the flora, fauna, and geology, pleading for people's respect. The arid rock provides a rare alvar habitat where only plants specifically adapted to the harsh climate of a naked stone surface survive. Delicate tiny herbs, lichens, and mosses find root-holds in the small fissures or, surprisingly, thick fleshy green-colored algae swell in the spring snow melt and rain that collects for a brief time in shallow depressions.

I liked the eerie surprise of happening upon a landscape left exactly as it was when the glacier left. Chattermarks show where hard rocks were dragged across the limestone surface, gouging out parallel crescents like phases of the moon. Some of these hard boulders remain, dropped across the plains 10,000 years ago but looking as though they were scattered last week. Some people, unable to resist leaving their own personal mark, apparently feel that they can improve on this wild landscape by stacking rocks into cairns. These unnatural changes jar like jolts of electricity, spoiling the natural beauty. The building of cairns is anathema to the "leave no trace" philosophy and is even illegal in Norway.

Ken Hatfield, a former geology professor at Lake Superior State University, understands geology geekism. One afternoon we sat in his living room overlooking the broad St. Mary's River. Ore boats moved slowly by and I felt the thrum of their engines as vibrations moved through the water and wet soil under the house. But what we marveled at was the fact that 10,000 years ago we would have been sitting beneath a mile thick layer of ice, so heavy that the earth is still rebounding from its weight, rising a foot per century. Astounding!

Much of Chippewa County is defined by that glacier. Its melt-water left a county so flat that the sky is the most remarkable scenery. The land was the bottom of great lakes where layers of silt settled sometimes hundreds of feet deep. It's fertile and grows good hay. New green grass sways and ripples like waves at sea. In mid-summer the hay is cut, rolled into fat round bales and shrink-wrapped in long caterpillar-like tubes of gleaming white plastic.

In early spring, water sits on top of this dense ground in shallow spring ponds that attract flocks of Canada geese and Sandhill cranes. If a field is left uncut, water-loving rushes and willows take over. This clay, technically silty clay loam, is so sticky that it'll suck the boots off anyone crazy enough to try to walk on it. Years ago a brick-making plant in the village of Rudyard made good use of this clay.

In winter, storms blow deep drifts across I-75, terrifying drivers when visibility is reduced to zero. On calmer days, snowy owls watch for mice from the tops of fence posts, glaring like small angry pillars of snow.

My father-in-law, Elmer Askwith, who grew up on that clay land, remembers how his bedroom window rattled when the wind raged across the open plains, blowing fine licks of snow onto his bed and floor. Elmer was seven when his family's well was drilled in the early 1920s. He remembered the hiccuping put-put of the driller's steam engine and the fact that the borehole went down through 300 feet of clay before it hit water. Water, under pressure from the clay above, gushed out of that hole in a non-stop stream. The well flowed for the next 75 years at least, continuing after his old home slumped away from that northwest wind and settled into the weeds.

One morning, news reached the health department about a flowing well that had gotten out of control. In trying to drill his own well, the home owner hit an aquifer under such intense pressure that it produced a geyser like air rushing out of a popped balloon. We all rushed out to the site, having heard exciting horror stories about out-of-control flowing wells. By the time we got there, the geyser had settled down but water continued to bubble from the ground, creating a lake among the trees and soil so soft that we feared the cabin might disappear into a giant sink-hole.

The Munuscong River flows through these clay flats, draining the fields eastward toward the St. Mary's River. The poet Stella-nova Osborn calls this river and other rivers, ditches, and areas of run-off, "fountains eternal."

I kayaked the river one summer afternoon, a lovely quiet ride, pushed along by the gentle current, experiencing a small flurry of excitement through faster ripples over fallen trees. The river was bordered on both sides by high banks, some showing the bare soil of newly eroded clay. The river was brown and dense with silt, too cloudy to see even a few inches below the surface.

One depression-era winter, Elmer worked on the St. Mary's River crew south of Sault Ste. Marie. It was a miserably cold job. By day, he helped map the river's depth, which changed as currents shifted silt on the river bottom, possibly obstructing shipping channels. At night, he slept in a canvas tent along the shore of the river, trying to stay warm under a thin blanket. The ten or twelve miles home was too far to drive twice a day, but he was grateful for the work.

Limestone, sometimes a repository for oil, sits below the clay in much of the county. That fact interested oil speculators in the early part of the twentieth century. They drilled exploratory oil wells on Neebish Island, St. Ignace, and especially in Pickford. "Day after day, week after week, the drilling progressed. Deeper and deeper went the hole. The village and surrounding population was aquiver with expectation. Down and down they went, one hundred feet, two hundred, then five hundred, then a thousand feet. Suspense was building up to enormous proportions."

The borehole cut through 119 feet of 10,000-year-old red glacial clay...through 128 feet of 405 to 425 million-year-old Niagara dolomitic limestone...through 265 feet of 500 million-year-old blue and black Ordovician shale...through 275 feet of white limestone...and 700 feet of Cambrian red rock up to 600 million years old. At various levels water poured forth in such quantities that the pounding of the drill amounted to little more than a common hammer blow.

Finally, drillers encountered "warm blood red" water under such pressure that it spurted twenty-five feet into the air, a water-spout visible throughout town. The water's pressure crushed the casing 1300 feet below grade. Thus ended the great search

for oil. But the well continued to gush water for the next hundred years, turning the ground around the well into a marshy wetland.

Tales of oil continued. "The oats I gave my horses for dinner were grown on our own farm and when the horses tried to chew them the oil oozed out of the grain," one grammar school student reported. And at least two farmers found the "black soapy substance that is characterized by oil men as the oil bearing substance" not far below the surface of their land. Not too many years ago, a local well driller encountered a pocket of crude oil in limestone. He filled one fifty-five-gallon drum before it petered out. He brought a Mason jar of it to our office. It looked exactly like what I poured into my lawn mower.

The glacier left stony ridges and also ponds that slowly become boggy swamps. I evaluated one such swamp bought by an excited new landowner who'd bought a hundred acres of this forested wetland. I stepped off the road and sank into soft sphagnum moss. Water covered my boots. We walked around, dodging spindly black spruce. Not hopeful signs for a drain field. I'd found a possible spot in my *Soil Maps*, a high ridge along the Waiska River. To get there we walked a half-mile along an old logging road over and around boggy ponds black with tannin and organic matter. A great blue heron balanced on a skinny leg and followed our progress with one yellow eye, head feathers erect and quivering. Mosquitoes pestered us, as usual. Eventually we found the ridge with soil that met the requirements, but the logistics of developing the site may have been too much. I never heard that he did anything with the property.

I was driving on a lonely road at the north side of Drummond Island on September 7, 2007, the day after the great opera singer Luciano Pavarotti died. The road was exceptionally rocky, hardly a road at all. Boulders and pools of water threatened my Pathfinder's undercarriage. I'd visited my Orthoceras (it hadn't been chipped away yet) and was headed toward an obscure beach strewn with peculiar chunks of limestone pitted with smooth holes.

Engraving - Porcupine Mountains

A red-tailed hawk soared low over the open limestone flats, looking for mice. A pair of Sandhill cranes stalked stiff-legged. I passed a dead snake so turquoise blue that the color seemed impossibly luminous. Heavy clouds glowered in the western sky and leaves of poplar trees shimmered frantically like the spangles of belly dancers. The air felt tense with the anticipation of a storm. The road entered a dark forest with green lacy ferns rising from a welter of fallen tree trunks just as NPR began playing the old recordings of Pavarotti. His perfect voice soared from the radio and my beloved Pathfinder felt like a cathedral, surrounded by shuddering trees, ancient and new life and death, and the coming storm. It truly felt like I was in the presence of God.

Leslie (Piastro Eger) Askwith has lived in the U.P. since 1976, working at the *Marquette Mining Journal* and Sault Tribe newspaper *Win Awenen Nisitotung*, and as a freelance writer for *Traverse Magazine* and *Lake Superior Magazine*. She published her own newspaper, *Homegrown,* for which she won a Communicator of the Year Award. She was the first writer-in-residence at Porcupine Mountains Wilderness State Park and won the Nature Writers of the Upper Peninsula contest in 2015. She recently completed a book called *Thunderstruck Fiddle: The Remarkable True Story of Charles Morris Cobb and His Hill Farm Community in 1850s Vermont.* She lives in Sault Ste. Marie and can be reached at leslieaskwith@hotmail.com

Silent Night

by Larry Buege, 4th Infantry Division 1967-68

Spider touches my shoulder and instantly I am awake. "It's two o'clock," he says.

I flick on a flashlight beneath my poncho and check my watch. Under the red light the dial on my watch confirms the time. It is not that I do not trust Spider, but it feels like I had just gotten to sleep. My watch begins at two. When my hour is up, I can return to sleep. Sleep is my escape from reality.

"Is anything going on?" I ask in a low whisper.

"Same-O, Same-O," he replies. "Nothing unusual."

"Did you do the radio check?"

"No."

Spider is wrapping himself in his poncho liner, showing no intention of making the call. I place the radio's receiver to my ear and key the mike.

"Sawbones 83 to Deadwood." I wait for a reply.

"Sawbones 83, this is Deadwood. Go ahead. Over."

"Sawbones 83 to Deadwood. How do you read us? Over."

"I read you lima charlie (loud and clear). Over."

"Sawbones 83...out."

I lean back against the trunk of a large bamboo tree and stare into the darkness. If they come, they will come from the front. Behind me, large bamboo shoots rise up like thick prison bars. With a sharp machete one might make fifty feet an hour. No, if they come, they will attack from the front where the land had once been cleared for farming. Tall grass has since reclaimed the clearing.

Spider is already breathing deeply in the early stages of sleep. War teaches one how to master sleep. Tonight I sleep in the grass at the edge of a bamboo thicket; two months ago it had been up against the still-warm foundation of a burned-out schoolhouse in downtown Pleiku—compliments of the Tet Offensive.

I again stare into the darkness. Anything beyond ten feet is little more than a shadow. My mind drifts off to the real world. It is exactly twelve hours away. At home it is also two o'clock. My father will be getting out of work early. My mother would normally be working as a waitress at a local diner, but she will have the day off. I have a brother in the Peace Corps in Panama. There is no telling what he might be doing. Loneliness begins to set in. Back home Christmas Eve is approaching. Over here every eve is the same.

"How can I be lonely with so many people around me?" you ask. "They are my friends," you say.

I am forced to acknowledge the wisdom of your argument. Around me are ten riflemen, a sergeant, and a newly minted second lieutenant. They are my friends. People back home assume we are fighting for our country—out of patriotism. What we fight for, when the bullets begin to fly, is not patriotism; it is for the guy in the foxhole beside us. That is what we fight for. It's as simple as that—nothing more. I will offer my life for the people beside me, as they will for me. Two days ago, before the recon patrol began, we had been strangers. I didn't even know their names. Now I do. One is named Spider, one is Juice, and we have a Tex. Every unit has a Tex. No matter what name I might have offered for myself, my name would be Doc. I am their medic. Those are all the names we need to know. Anything more is superfluous.

Perhaps loneliness is not the best term to express my feelings. Perhaps it is deeper than that—more a feeling of insignificance. I look above me. In a gap of the bamboo shoots I see a portion of the sky with its endless stars. The cleared area on the ground in front of me appears to zoom out like a cheap Hollywood movie stunt. It soon disappears, and the globe of the earth materializes. That, too, becomes smaller as the camera continues its outward zoom until the earth is only a speck, a small blue dot in some inconspicuous corner of the universe. I can now see myself from the viewpoint of the stars that have been shining down on earth for eternity.

"In the realm of the endless and eternal universe...do you believe a man sitting at the edge of a clearing with an M-16 in his lap really makes a difference?" the stars ask.

I can offer no reply.

In the sky that hangs loosely over the clearing are more stars. One of them is moving toward me. It has to be a plane or helicopter. At this time of night, it is more likely the former. A mile south of me, it begins to circle. I see the glowing, orange ribbon first. It looks like a streamer of crepe paper someone is waving in the night sky. But its fiery brilliance is breathtaking. Seconds later the sound reaches my ears. It is a low moan, like a painful wail from some mythical monster.

The Air Force calls them AC-47s, twin-engine planes equipped with three mini-guns each capable of spitting out 6,000 rounds a minute. Those of us unfortunate enough to have seen them in action from the ground called them "Spooky" or "Puff the Magic Dragon."

I watch the plane circle around spitting out its tracer fire. On the last round, it comes within 1,000 yards of our position. I key the mike on our radio.

"Sawbones 83 to Deadwood, over."

"Sawbones 83, this is Deadwood. Go ahead, over."

"Be advised we have Spooky at our doorstep. Does he know we're here? Does he have our coordinates? Over."

"Wait one, Sawbones 83...."

I visualize Deadwood back at base camp with his feet upon some desk. He will have a coffee mug in his left hand and will now be reaching for a sandwich with his right. After he has taken a couple of bites, he will pick up the landline and place a call to whoever is in charge of Spooky. It might not be fair, but that is the image lodged in my mind.

"Sawbones 83, this is Deadwood. Over."

"Deadwood, this is Sawbones 83. We're still here. We're not going anywhere."

"Be advised S-2 (military intelligence) has reason to believe Charlie is visiting your sector. Spooky was dispatched in your honor. When he leaves, they'll place H and I rounds (harassment and interdiction) around your perimeter to keep Charlie honest."

"Roger that, Deadwood. Sawbones 83, out."

I hope my voice sounded calm and professional over the radio. It is not the way I feel. One small error and Spooky will be raining bullets down upon us like a summer hailstorm. Friendly fire won't even earn a purple heart. Does a wound from friendly fire hurt less? I wonder how well our lieutenant scored in his map-reading class at OCS.

I wait in the darkness, watching Puff do her thing. The ribbons of fire created by the tracers are almost a work of art as they lace through the night sky, but the moaning sound is unsettling, sending a chill through my body. It reminds me of the song "They Call the Wind Maria" from the musical *Paint Your Wagon*. How does that verse go?... "Maria makes the mountains sound like folks was out there dying."

"Is someone out there dying under that deluge of gunfire?" I wonder. Maybe no one will ever know.

"If someone in a woods cries out in pain and there is no one there to hear his cry, does he still suffer pain?" I ask.

"That's stupid," I reply. "The pain is just as real."

Engraving - S.S. Ironside

"Must you two always bicker?" a third voice says.

"Yes, we must," they reply in unison.

They are both right, of course—each in his own way. Somewhere, as I sit here in the dark, a woman is being raped. Not a sensual sex act, but a brutal, violent attack that is every bit as traumatic as anything this war has to offer. Somewhere, there is a young child suffering pain from the terminal stages of cancer. Somewhere, there is a mother or wife receiving a notice from a military chaplain. But I do not know them; therefore, they do not exist. They never happened.

"That is precisely the point I was trying to make," I say.

"But it's still real to the people involved," I reply.

It is obvious those two are not about to let it rest. I don't know why I put up with them. Spider doesn't suffer from such conflicts. He described his hour as "nothing unusual."

I lay my M-16 on the ground and reach into my rucksack for what remains of my dinner. It is a can of ham and lima beans from the C-ration pack. It has no commercial value, as it cannot be traded for anything. It is literally the bottom of the food chain, but when you're hungry, you'll eat anything. I open the can with my P-38 can opener and scoop out the contents with my plastic spoon. It isn't the tastiest meal, but it gives me something to do and prevents my mind from wandering.

I finish the beans with a polite, but subdued, burp and toss the can to the side. I will have to pick it up in the morning—nothing will be left to confirm our existence. By then it will be daylight. We will be able to see what we are doing.

I reach for my M-16 with my right hand—it isn't there. I am overtaken with panic. My heart races within my chest, and I begin to hyperventilate. With both hands I begin patting the ground. It only takes a moment or two to find the weapon, but my heart continues to race. I hold it close to my chest. I don't know why. My M-16 is still a virgin. I have never fired it in anger. Hopefully, I never will. Every time the fecal matter hits the proverbial fan, a medic is too busy to need a weapon. Still, it is my security blanket and I need it. I have dreams at night about losing my gun. Some people have dreams about having no clothes. I have dreams about having no gun. I am sure other people do not share such dreams. Sometimes I worry about my mental stability. Even emotionally stable people have cracked during wartime.

I clutch my M-16 to my chest like a mother clutching an infant just rescued from perilous danger; then I feel foolish. I pull my poncho over my head and turn on my flashlight: it is two-thirty. My watch is half done.

I stare into the darkness for another ten minutes. In the darkness, there is nothing to see. With no wind, there is nothing to hear. Except for the lingering smell of ham and lima beans, there is nothing to smell. A university psychology department could not have constructed a better sensory-deprivation lab. It is good, but not perfect. About every five minutes, an artillery shell falls around our perimeter. They do provide more personal space than Spooky did; none fall closer than half a mile. No one in our squad is even awakened.

Those noises I can overlook. Those noises I can understand. What is disconcerting are the occasional noises in front of me. They are subtle to be sure, perhaps just my imagination. A lonely watch can do that to you. If someone else were present, the noise would qualify for a "Did you hear that?" Nothing more.

Sometimes the noises are real, but that does not make them sinister. Every land has its share of wildlife capable of creating noises in the night. I stare at the distant shadows—they appear to be moving. I rub my eyes and look again. Sometimes when there is no background for reference, objects appear to move. Psychologists call it auto-kinesis. The shadows continue to move. I focus on two shadows, paying particular attention to the space between them—the space remains constant. The movement is probably my imagination.

On the practical side, it would make no difference if they were real. We are a recon team. We are to avoid contact at all costs. We are motionless and silent. We have trees at our back, eliminating visible shadows. We will see them long before they see us.

What would happen if I did come face-to-face with my counterpart? Would I hesitate? Would he hesitate? Our country has been in many wars. All our old enemies are now our friends. Can I kill a man tonight who tomorrow could have been my friend? If I were to pretend I don't see him, would he pretend he doesn't see me and walk away?

I push my thoughts into the far recesses of my brain, but they are like articles of clothing in an over-stuffed suitcase—they resist closure.

I remain in place leaning against my bamboo backrest and give the chimerical bogey the rite of passage. The next fifteen minutes are uneventful. I again crawl under my poncho to check the time: It is now five minutes to three; my watch is almost over. I key the mike on the radio. It is time for our hourly radio check.

"Sawbones 83 to Deadwood." There is no answer.

"Sawbones 83 to Deadwood." I again wait for a reply.

"Sawbones 83, this is Deadwood. Go ahead, over."

I can hear radio music in the background. Deadwood obviously does not get as much fresh air as we do.

"Sawbones 83 to Deadwood, how do you read us, over?"

"I read you lima charlie, over."

"Sawbones 83, out."

It should now be three o'clock. I crawl over to Juice and touch him on the shoulder. He is instantly awake.

"It's three o'clock...time for your shift," I whisper.

Juice rubs his eyes in hopes it will help him see into the darkness; it does not.

"Anything happen on your shift?" he asks.

"Same-O, Same-O," I reply, "Nothing unusual."

Larry Buege's short stories have received regional and international (English) awards. He has also authored eight novels including the ever-popular *Chogan Native American Series*. More information about his novels can be found at Amazon.com, Gastropod-publishing.com, or by contacting the author directly at LSBuege@aol.com.

Au Train Rising

by Mikel B. Classen

Entering Au Train, MI

A cross the Upper Peninsula there are many small communities; most struggle daily to survive. Some don't succeed and fall away in time as historical footnotes. Au Train (see Fig. 1) is one of those small towns, or so it seemed a few years ago, but in recent years, the town is on the rise.

For a century, Au Train has depended on its natural beauty for its lifeblood. Au Train Lake, the Au Train River, and the sand beaches of Au Train Bay on Lake Superior made for a powerful lure in the early 1900s. Resorts sprang up and the one-time logging town became a tourist destination. It has remained so to this day, but in the late '90s and early 2000s, it appeared the community was on its last legs. Resorts were for sale, and the few businesses that remained either barely eked out a living or failed completely.

Suddenly Au Train is transforming. Not away from the nice small town it always has been but into a recreational destination once again. As one shopkeeper put it, "When kay-

aking became popular in Munising and Pictured Rocks, they found us too."

The Au Train River (see Fig. 2), the Au Sable of the Upper Peninsula, has always been the best river in the U.P. for a float for a canoe or a kayak. Even pontoon boats cruise it periodically. Not only is it fairly large and wide, but it connects Au Train Lake with Lake Superior. When it leaves Au Train Lake, the river meanders under Forest Lake road. It then meanders for several miles and then goes under Forest Lake Road again, not even a mile from where it crossed before. Then it flows for a few more miles into Lake Superior, again barely a mile from where it crossed before. It doesn't get more paddle friendly than that. You can take the river in pieces, or you can go for the big paddle and start at the Au Train Lake Campground and paddle all of Au Train Lake and the River.

Au Train Lake Campground is a US Forest Service campground and is located on the south end of Au Train Lake. This is a thirty-two-site campground that is primitive, no hookups, and vault bathrooms though they are well taken care of and nice. There is also a boat launch for public access to Au Train Lake and the River. Like many USFS camp-grounds, there are no ATVs allowed though the area has an intricate ATV trail system and Au Train itself is quite ATV friendly.

The Au Train Lake Campground also con-tains the Au Train Songbird Trail. This was something that was developed by the Michi-gan Department of Natural Resources, US Forest Service Hiawatha National Forest, and lots of local folks. This is a two-mile in-terpretive hiking trail through UP forest that eventually follows an incredibly picturesque stream. There are signs depicting local song-birds and how to recognize them. The local stores have a tape for sale that has each of the bird calls from the signs that are meant to be played along the trail with the signs.

Alger County is famous for its waterfalls and Au Train has them, too. The turnoff for Au Train Falls runs east and is about 100 feet before M-94 when traveling south on Forest Lake Road. It is poorly marked but worth looking for. There are two sets of falls. The lower falls (see Fig. 3) are the easiest to access and the one most viewed. The upper falls have a degree of "Am I crazy trying to get to these falls?" The slope leading down to it is very steep and fit for mountain goats. Naturally, I had to investigate. South of the upper falls, the Au Train River is dammed and the steel spillway runs across the upper falls past the lower for some of the area's hy-droelectricity. This can make the upper falls seem like they aren't flowing well, but the lower falls are flowing hard. As I stood at the bottom of the upper falls, I saw no less than six small streams, all coming from springs in the surrounding rock flowing hard feed-ing the Au Train River. This small cradle of life, refused to be beaten by logging and dams, still flowed making the Au Train one of the clearest rivers in Michigan.

With cars lining the road at access points to the river, the town of Au Train seems to be prospering. The Northwoods Resort has set up shop at the river crossings renting ca-noes and spotting paddlers. They are even getting into Fat Bike rentals. The amazing thing to me was the lunch truck they had set up along the river at one of the pull-out points. Let me repeat that: *there is a lunch truck parked daily along the Au Train River!* The food isn't bad either.

The food isn't bad anywhere in Au Train. The Au Train Grocery makes good meaty pasties daily. They also serve subs, but I couldn't get past the pasties. The A&L Party Store, the first place you see when you come into Au Train, serves an excellent pizza by any standards and oven-baked subs that were being made here in Au Train long be-fore Quiznos and those other chains thought of it. When I met my wife, many moons ago, she lived in Au Train and we ate here on a regular basis. It's still as good and it's still owned by the same family. Actually, my sub was cooked by the very same person.

The real surprise for me was Wegener's Café and Deli. Where did this place come from and how did it end up in Au Train? They serve schnitzel! For those that don't know, schnitzel is a Bavarian dish that is es-sentially a pounded piece of pork and then breaded lightly and cooked until the bread is crispy. Traditionally, veal is used instead of pork, but it is excellent with pork. This unas-suming little restaurant is Bavarian cuisine based with hot dogs and burgers thrown in to appeal to the mainstream. They serve Jager, a tasty German gravy, and meatballs. Their salads are Bavarian based and Ger-man potato salad is made in season. They even serve sauerkraut as a side. Think about that in a small tent with someone you don't like. The other attraction of this place is their bakery. I had a raspberry handpie, basically a turnover, with a cup of coffee. That's how you finish a day right. This place is unique enough in the U.P. that I would turn into Au Train just for Wegener's.

Au Train is one of the oldest place names along the Lake Superior coastline (See Fig. 4). It was the site of Native American fish-ing and home of the legendary "Face in the Rock." Then a fur trading post. When School-craft County was reorganized to create Alger County, Au Train was the first county seat. It was home of one of the first U.P. newspapers, the *Au Train Alpha*. At one time nearly 1000 people lived around Au Train. Some of the

Old log cabin overlooks the meandering Au Train River near Lake Superior

Au Train Lake Meets Au Train River

Lower Au Train Falls

old homes of Au Train still reflect those early days, and where the railroad once ran, ATVs now follow the old route.

It seems fitting that a place of such antiquity should continue to rise up and thrive in spite of the odds of the modern world. Those who have lived in the U.P. know what it is. The Finns called it "Sisu." It's the refusal to quit when everything else says you should. Whether Au Train found life or life found Au Train, it really doesn't matter. What matters is Au Train is rising. How far or how long remains to be seen, but right now the odds are looking good.

Mikel Classen has been writing about northern Michigan in newspapers and magazines for over thirty-five years, creating feature articles about the history, travel, outdoors, and culture of Michigan's North Country. A journalist, historian, photographer, and author with a fascination for the world around him, he enjoys researching and writing about lost stories from the past. To learn more about him and to see more of his work, check out his website http://mikelclassen.com.

Bear Woman

by Ann Dallman

Most people see her as a middle-aged woman. They are blind to her true nature. She is a black bear and I want her.

She's had several mates. Strong yet foolishly proud, they wander off from her woods. She's faced her share of adversity. This is character building, yet emotionally draining.

For years she has prowled for work and sustenance. Sniffing, snuffling, and not really seeing. Vision is difficult and limited for a black bear. The same is true of her human form when looking for men. Eventually, her satisfaction is limited to caring for her cubs and indulging her sweet tooth. Summer yields berries...sweet, ripe, and moist in the early-morning sun...gleaming and waiting. Fall brings its bounty of apples...easy to find as they drop from the sky. The human in her dreams of making applesauce, the bear in her of eating it.

In her human form, she confided in me.

"I dreamt of bears last night as they shape shifted into the coyote trickster," she said. "When I woke, I offered my tears and breaking heart to the Creator. I begged to be healed of this heartbreak."

I bring her gifts of honey and maple syrup. She smiles her thanks showing her teeth. For the briefest minute I see a snout, but look again and realize it is her face. She sniffs the gifts in appreciation.

Winters lulls her with its cold temperatures and beckoning caves. Her body temperature drops, her metabolism slows down, and she sleeps. Her dreams promise her that someday she will find her mate.

Time passes. She encounters health problems in both her forms—human and bear. The human in her suffers with each monthly cycle. She reverts into her stoic bear nature to endure the pain. Her days of bearing offspring—whether human or animal—are ending.

"Your hand? It's in a cast," she said to me one day as I walked into work. "What happened?"

"Must have caught it in a trap," I replied knowing that she would understand.

"You should be more careful. We're not getting any younger; those days are winding down." As she turned to leave me, I noticed the gray starting to appear in her hair. And, for the first time, I notice its coarseness.

She endures the death of her friend, Teddy, a black bear. He has spent twenty years on land, on this Mother Earth, and his internal organs have disintegrated. The end comes slowly. She grieves for her loss. We learned of his passing on a spring day filled with the promise of the sun's warmth. Later that week we traveled with a medicine man to a wildlife refuge and now the site of Teddy's grave. There the earth was shaped into a mound to cover Teddy's remains.

The medicine man was dressed in jeans, a dark blue work shirt, and cowboy boots. He held a ceremonial staff in his left hand. Eagle feathers tied to its top danced in the wind. He spoke words of blessing in Ojibway for Teddy. He bent to scatter tobacco over the makeshift grave. The medicine man's words filled the air and then ended. My friend, the one I hold closest in my heart, wiped her tears and turned to leave. I followed her to my car.

"Let's drive a bit and then you can drop me off near my resting spot in the woods. I need to be alone." I did as she asked and then I drove off.

We took our breaks together that next day at work. We sat outdoors on a cement ledge and nursed our bottles of water. There was no need for words. I looked at her. She noticed my gaze and returned my look. She shrugged her shoulders and looked down. She dragged her foot against the ledge to make a soft scraping "scrrch." At almost the same time we started to sniff the air. Ah, someone was intruding on our silence and moving into our space. A coworker rushed toward us with news of a car accident.

"A truck driver down the road slammed into a bear as it crossed the back highway. The truck's in bad shape but the driver is okay. The bear is dead."

We watched as other coworkers hearing of the news scrambled for their cars. Each wanted to claim the meat. But not for us. We don't eat our own kind.

A few days later she wore eyeglasses for the first time.

"Well, you know how it is. We can smell just fine but we don't see so well."

I agreed with her as I pushed my own eyewear up the bridge of my nose.

The next day she told me of an unusual occurrence. "I talked to one of my neighbors before I left for work this morning. He told me he spotted a black bear pawing the ground underneath my bedroom window last night. I think it's a sign."

That next week a new mate came to her. It's not me. This male says he is attracted by the sweetness of her body's unique scent. And, like a hibernating bear licking its own pads, he now licks her feet. He says it helps to nourish him through his own time of sleep. Or maybe it is just the closeness to her body that he needs.

"Yes. The sign told me he would come," she told me. I looked away so she wouldn't see my sadness.

This new mate watches her as she pads upright down the long corridors at work. As a man, his vision is acute. He tells her that he knew from the very beginning that they would be together.

"Ah," she tells him, "so males know these things too."

He brushes at her. "Yes, Little Bear Woman, I know of these things."

During their evenings together they feast on salmon and smoked fish. They avoid fast food. They avoid hunters. It is the season to kill their kind and many men now roam the woods armed with powerful guns. Her new mate is successful at avoiding them. He knows their favorite spots and shudders with their shouts. I wonder if they pant when they are together. Do they make the huffing sounds of our kind or are they quiet in the way of some humans? I stop pondering this to ramble off, to forage for a meal.

I watch and wait throughout their courtship which is long in human years. Part of me hopes they stay together, part of me waits for it to end.

Note: The black bear is the only species of bear found in Michigan according to the Department of Natural Resources. The department estimates the adult bear population to be 9,700 individuals in the Upper Peninsula and about 2,000 in the Lower Peninsula. It's not unusual to come across a bear or two while driving around our backwoods. An encounter on a state highway early one morning as the sun rose led to many thoughts about that bear, which eventually led to this story. I like to think it has a happy ending.

Ann Dallman is the content editor of *Tri-City Neighbors* magazine focusing on the residents of Marinette and Peshtigo (WI) and Menominee (MI). A former English teacher, she edited, wrote, and did the graphic design for *Sam English: The Life, Work and Times of An Artist* (2009 Coffee Table Book of the Year/PEAK Award). A former newspaper editor, she has also published in national trade magazines. The Society of Children's Book Writers and Illustrators/Michigan Chapter named her as Runner Up in its 2016 Multicultural Mentorship Competition.

Superior Sailing

by Deborah K. Frontiera

I was about twelve years old when my parents decided to purchase a thirty-three foot fiberglass sailboat with teak decking. It was an exciting event at that age—camping on a boat, sailing all over Lake Superior, having adventures at sea. After all, I was already a seasoned sailor because we had what my dad referred to as a "Barnegat Bay Sneak Box," a shallow-draft sailboat about fourteen feet long with a large centerboard and a gaff rig, which I had already learned to maneuver around the "arm" of Portage Lake that is referred to as Bootjack. I knew how to handle a tiller and keep a mostly straight course, bring the main sail sheet in or let it out to catch the best wind, and how much of a slant that little vessel could handle before one had to slack off on the sheet to avoid capsizing. The feel of that point and riding on a steep slant let me experience that certain "high" that pre-teens and teens love.

In 2001, after the death of my mother, I asked my father if he still had the logbook from that boat. He did, and gave it to me. It sat in a box waiting for me to retire and have time to read it. That read, which finally happened during the spring of 2016—eight years after I retired from my teaching job—brought back a flood of memories. It made me realize the numerous times that Lake Superior held our lives in her waves and winds as she always has over the long history of people venturing out onto her waters. Many of those sailors did not survive to tell their tales about our shark-free, salt-free,

The "Lorelei" at Sail

but often hypothermia-inducing-cold inland ocean.

Technically, a logbook simply states what time a ship left harbor, course and wind direction, latitude and longitude along the way, and arrival time at its destination. When I read my father's handwriting, I read a true log book. My mother's log notes were much more than that. I've selected some portions to share in the hope that you, too, can feel as though you are out on Gitche Gumee, either in the present time, or some time long gone by. The lake has lessons to teach those who listen.

Fall 1963

"Sloop *Lorelei* (see Fig. 1) arrived at Portage Entry on Sep. 21, 1963, traveling by flat-bed truck from Costa Mesa, California. She was put in the water, masted, and had her shakedown cruise on Sep. 22nd, 1963, and delivered to our hands on that date.

"Our first sail included Clarke, Celia [my parents], Pearce, Kathy, Betsy [siblings], Debbie, and John Umbarger [Kathy's boyfriend and later husband] as crew and consisted of a brief and hectic run out on Keweenaw Bay during which we attempted to cook and eat a chicken dinner. Among other things, we discovered that a new motor makes a bad smell, that sailboats tend to be on a severe slant much more than upright and that all equipment should be tied or bolted down, especially stoves."

I laughed to think my mother had not anticipated the slant—she'd been on that Barnegat Bay Sneak Box with my father numerous times—and had capsized it on their first sail. Maybe she thought only small sailboats slanted, but thirty-three feet, while it might seem huge, is still small. My father, who taught math and mining engineering at Michigan Tech University, solved the stove problem by putting a screw on each side of the "stove well" and hanging it on a wire cable so it swung back and forth staying level as the boat tipped. He also modified the shelves inside the cupboards and storage spaces so they did not pop open while out on the water.

"The return trip through the Keweenaw waterway was much smoother and we anchored safely at the buoy at the Cabin [our summer home made of logs in the Finnish tradition] after dark, making a spectacular arrival with cabin and spreader lights ablaze. From this date until she went into winter storage on Nov. 3, we enjoyed mainly day sails and had beautiful fall weather throughout this time. We spent one night aboard, anchored in front of the Cabin—

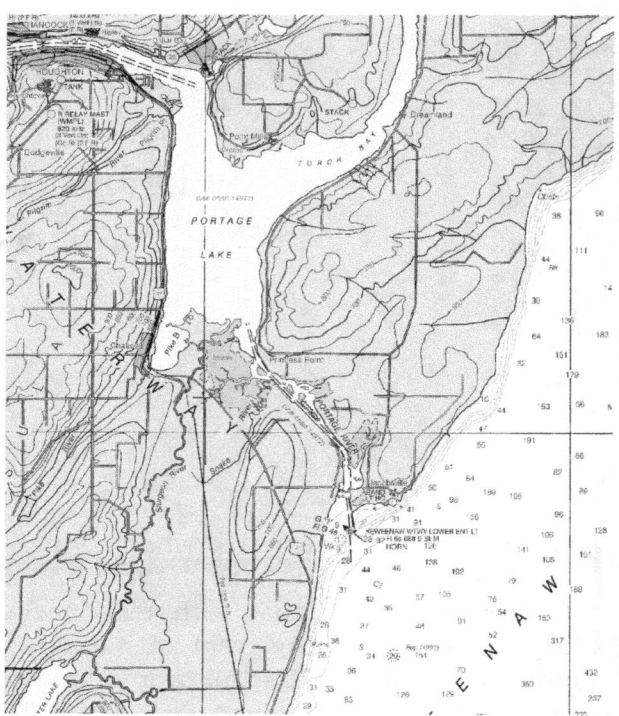

Keweenaw waterway: Portage Lake to Keweenaw Bay

and that was enough as it got so cold that the moisture condensed on the ceiling and dripped on us all night; the light system failed; and it rained."

Lorelei slept six. My parents had the "captain's cabin" in a v-shaped double bunk in the bow, with a door to separate it from the main cabin. The booth/table in the galley/main cabin area dropped down and had a cushion put over it to sleep two more. Two slept in little tunnel/caves that ran under the cockpit benches above. One of those little caves was mine. Cold drops of water woke me in the wee hours of that night—moisture from my own breath, condensed and coming back to me. I buried my head inside my sleeping bag and longed for morning to come. Camping on a boat was not all it was cracked up to be. But by the following summer, I was ready for more adventures and would always keep my nose inside my sleeping bag.

July 9, 1964

"Betsy, Debbie, Clarke, and Celia set sail from the Cabin at 10 a.m. motoring to the Entry as breeze was light to non-existent. It was a very warm, sunny day with light SE winds across Keweenaw Bay which died completely near Point Abbaye. We motored the remainder of the day, circling the Huron Islands (rugged and beautiful) disturbing nesting seagulls and swimming baby gulls. Drifted and swam off islands, then proceeded to Pine River area where we went ashore for hamburgers on charcoal. [We had a dingy—small boat with oars and a 3-horse-power motor—tied to *Lorelei* and floating behind—used to go ashore when anchored anywhere.] Beautiful beach homes in this area which we found later were part of the Huron Mountain Club. Arrived Big Bay at 8:30, warmly welcomed by local inhabitants and tourists. [At that time, *Lorelei* was one of the few pleasure sailing vessels on Lake Superior. We were a novelty.] Excellent facilities (shower and bathrooms, electricity, water, gasoline, etc.). This was a beautiful day and trip—shoreline, hills, cliffs and beaches were lovely although dimmed by heat haze. Huron Island light, looking like a church, was most picturesque."

Ah, this trip was more like what I'd had in mind.

July 10, 1964

"Left Big Bay at 8:15 with moderate west wind, under sail, headed for Marquette or Munising—destination indefinite. Winds became southeast so we decided to head for Munising on a course of 115°. Horizon was hazy so visibility wasn't too clear. We crossed the path of one freighter near Granite Rock, but otherwise saw no one. From Granite Rock at 11:20 until we saw Grand Island at 4:50 we were out of sight of land. Thanks to our navigator, we were on course and on time. Winds changed and became light at Grand Island so we motored in to Munising anchoring for supper near the tip of one of the outlying small islands. Arrived Munising at 8:10, moored at the public dock which offers safe anchorage but no facilities—and lots of sightseers. Business districts only one block away—ice, beer, groceries, etc. available."

July 11, 1964

"Left Munising at 5:30 a.m. under motor, headed for Pictured Rocks. Passed Castle Rock at 6 a.m. and Clarke got the family up to look. Shoreline is very rugged and beautiful—should be seen in afternoon to get full effect. Many cave formations, interesting formations, towering cliffs and many colors. [I viewed the cliffs as giant, multi-layered, peanut-butter-and-jelly sandwiches with the jelly oozing out some of the layers.] Slightly obscured by haze on this day. Heavy sea swells, but no wind. Motored back to Grand Island, hoisted sail and ran into fog. The remainder of the day we had intermittent fog although it generally hugged the shore. Took a straight course for Marquette, wind

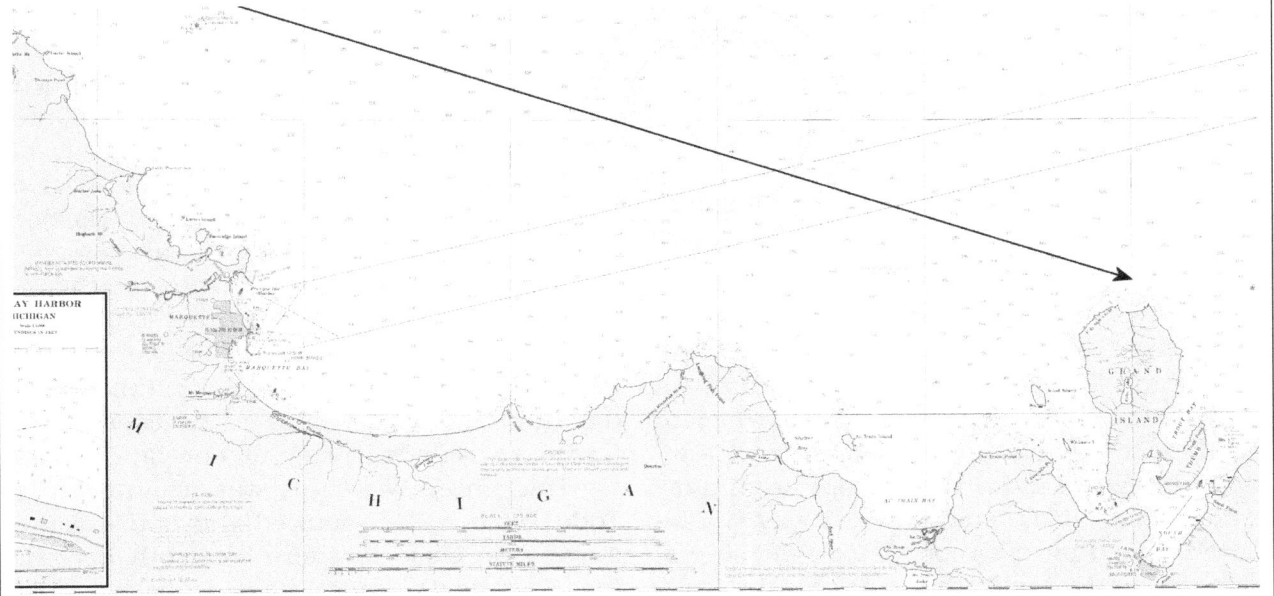

Granite Rock to Grand Island

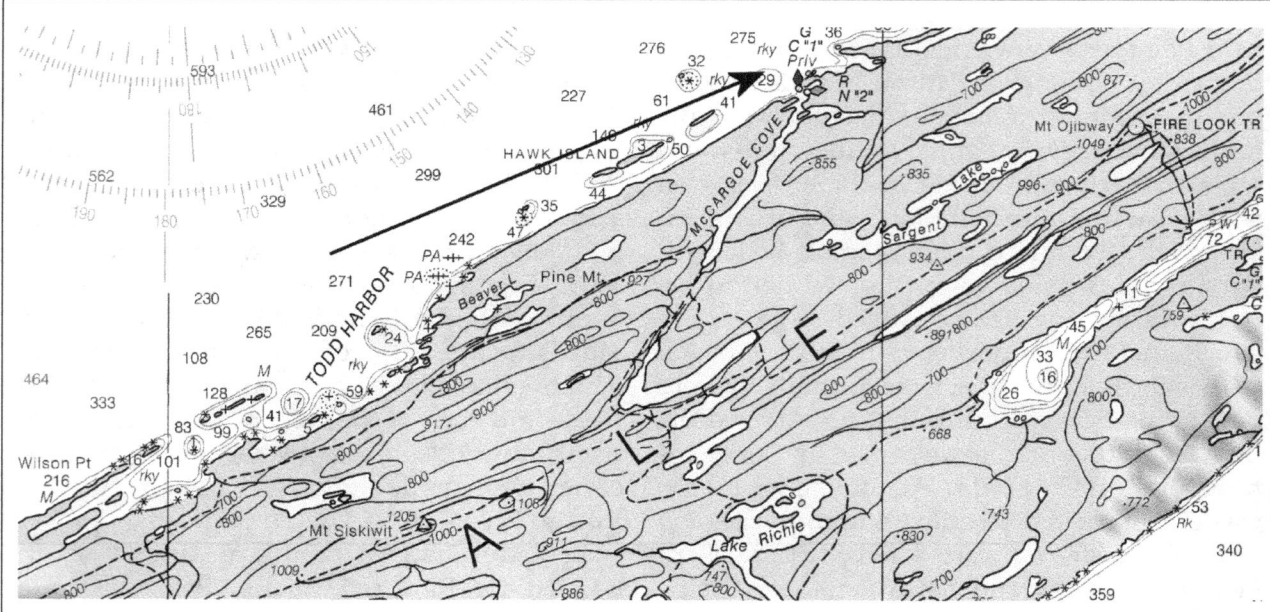

Todd Harbor to McCargoe Cove

from NW which steadily freshened through the day and seas increased. Shoreline obscured nearly all the way but fog lifted as we approached Marquette. Had to drop Genoa and hoist working jib—and Celia, Betsy and Debbie were all experiencing *mal de mer* [seasickness]. As we approached Marquette, sea became very rough. We all got wet and were glad to moor at Marquette. Wonderful facilities. Fresh water also at dock. Took wet clothes to laundromat to dry out and entertained many interested visitors.

"On Sunday we prepared for a rough return trip but sea beyond the breakwater was too rough. Estimated at least 8 ft. waves, and we returned to Marquette. Pearce picked us up for return drive and *Lorelei* was left moored for several days."

For those not familiar with how waves are measured, it's from a *flat* sea, so an eight-foot wave is sixteen feet from trough to crest! My mother was practically hysterical when we got beyond the breakwater. Undaunted, Dad, Betsy, and I pressed on, but finally admitted the need to turn back. I boasted that I could easily go to the bow and get that jib down, and, no thank you, I didn't need a rope around my waist—invincible teenager that I was. My father insisted on the rope. It took me several minutes to fight with that sail—all the while rising and falling sixteen to twenty feet with

each wave! My father fought with the tiller all that time to keep us turned into the wind to prevent capsizing. Down in each trough, looking up at a wall of water that seemed like it would crash down on my head at any moment, scared the beegeebers out of me. I've never been so properly humbled by the powers of nature on Lake Superior. It wasn't until I was in my late fifties, having a good laugh with my dad (in his early nineties) that I admitted I almost wet my pants that day.

"Return trip was made on July 15 and 16 with Clarke, Pearce, Bob Garieppy and Tom Hruby aboard. An uneventful trip was reported except for millions of black flies which plagued them and Pearce's suffering from a bout of the flu. They stayed at Big Bay enroute."

July 22, 1965—our first trip to Isle Royale
"During our stay at Washington Harbor weather was cool, cloudy and partly foggy. We left about 10:30 in uncertain weather—haze and threatening fog. After looking at the weather outside the harbor, we decided to proceed but kept careful log times and distances along the route. At times we were forced to reduce speed to one-quarter as fog thickened. Worst fog was around Little Todd Harbor. We motored the entire route staying as close to shore as depth permitted. Our depth finder was invaluable both as safety feature and as navigational aid as

we established our position several times by depth reading. Fog lifted in time for a pleasant passage from Todd Harbor (where we entered with a view of staying and waiting out the fog—but no dock) to McCargoe Cove. We docked about 4 p.m.—weather very warm, sunny and delightful."

Lorelei had all the "latest" equipment: ship-to-shore radio, dingy/lifeboat, depth finder, floating compass, etc. My father was also experienced with a sextant. I've often thought back to the early days of shipping on the Great Lakes when a compass, sextant, and "spyglass" were all the technology available. When the weather can shift so much in a few hours, it's a wonder that there were not even more shipwrecks back in those days. Technology today is even greater, yet there are still boating accidents and drownings each year. Have we become so dependent on devices that we forget common sense?

July 24 Saturday

"Left McCargoe Cove at 10:07 under sail with light NW wind, clear, sunny and beautiful. Wind died shortly and we motored through Amygdaloid Channel, then around Belle Isle and into Robinson Bay. Slight breeze enabled us to sail down the bay, trailing, and on into Picard Cove where we found a small bay to the left of the channel. We anchored here— a delightful spot—had lunch and swam for a short time. A beautiful following wind from Picard Cove to the northeast end of Robinson Bay made a beautiful sail. Strong breeze from there to entrance of Duncan Bay made fast sailing. The narrows of Duncan Bay is very shallow—one should keep far to the left of the rocks and continue well until rocks are past. We hit bottom and bumped along but didn't get hung up. We moored at the far campground of Duncan Bay about 6 p.m.—a remote and quiet spot."

July 27, 1964

"Left Chippewa Harbor at 7:20 a.m. under clear skies with light NW wind which increased slightly. Set SE course of 135° for Copper Harbor and sailed throughout. Estimated speed 5-6 mph. At 9 a.m., 8 miles off shore, we changed course to 150° headed for Eagle Harbor. A tiny bird appeared from nowhere (it looked like a chickadee but had a yellow breast) and flew right into the cabin where it perched on a curtain. After a short time it came out, sat on a cockpit cushion with us, then perched on a stay, then flew off again toward Isle Royale. Wind gradually increased throughout the afternoon in general from SW. We kept at 140° later, deciding to go to Copper Harbor after all, as fog turned out to be a mirage. Seas increased during the afternoon and it was very cold. Arrived in Copper Harbor at 4:15—excellent time from the island. Left *Lorelei* at the Marina and drove home."

We often drove in two cars, leaving one at some marina or other, while other family members brought the boat to that place. It saved time later on and allowed us to have longer excursions in short stages. We always had someone we could call upon to come and get us in an emergency as you will see in the next episode.

August 22, 1965—I was not part of the crew on this cruise—probably had summer band practice or something. This section of the log book also illustrates the vast difference between my mother's log entries and those of my father.

"Left the Cabin at 5:15 p.m. with Clarke, Pearce, Kathy, John and Jim aboard bound for the Apostle Islands.

Heading 300° @ 9 p.m. Sun. Aug. 22. Speed 4 knots

Heading 310° @ 9:20 p.m. Sun. Aug 22. Speed 4 knots

Heading 260° @ 9:40 p.m. Aug. 22. Speed 6.75 mph, 2 1/3 miles out from light [guessing the light referred to is at the "Lilly Pond" on west end of Portage Canal]

Heading 270° @ 11:10 p.m. Sun. Aug. 22. Speed 3 knots

Heading 260° @ 12:05 a.m. Mon. Aug. 23

Heading 260° @ 12:50 a.m. Speed 3 knots

Heading 260° @ 6 a.m. Mon. Aug. 23 speed 3; 33.5 miles from 9:40 p.m. Sun.

Heading 240° @ 6:200 a.m. Mon. Speed 5 knots

Heading 240° @ 9:30 a.m. Mon. Aug. 22. Speed 5 knots

Heading 250° @ 10 a.m. Speed 5 knots

Heading 320° @ 11 a.m. Speed 3 knots

"We arrived at Bayfield [Wisconsin] at 7:15 p.m. and looked at boats in the yacht club.

Spent the night at public dock and in the morning around 10, we left to cruise the islands. When we got about to Bass Island we had an unfortunate acci————-"

The pen ran out of ink at that point and no more was written about that trip. I called my sister Kathy at her home in Washington State on May 23, 2016, to find out what happened. They were running downwind and decided to put up the Genoa Jib in addition to the regular jib and the mainsail so they could have "balloons" out front for the wind. Pearce was gathering up sail and tossing it back. When he got to the end, there was a metal eyelet for the rope to go through. When he tossed it, it hit Kathy in the mouth, breaking one front tooth and jamming the other up. They went back to Bayfield where someone—Kathy couldn't remember but probably Mom—picked up Kathy to take her to a dentist for the teeth to be capped. John went with Kathy. The others on board continued the cruise, but left no written record.

Sept. 10, 1966, another near-disaster of which I was not a part because the school year had begun. Again, these were my father's log notes.

"Began week cruise 11:55 p.m. from Copper Harbor. Clarke, Cort Olson, Jim Wescoat, Jim Enrietti. Cleared Copper Harbor bell at 12:30 p.m. with 25 mph SE wind.

Sept. 11, 1966

"Arrived at north entrance to Rock Harbor, Isle Royale 9 a.m. Docked about 9:30 a.m. Visibility was not good but adequate. In p.m. motored to Daisy Farm and back with a short stop at Mott Island.

Sept. 12, 1966

"Fog all day. Lifted some by noon. Motored to Mc-Cargoe Cove. Moored at Bush Island at 5 p.m.

Sept. 13, 1966

"Left McCargoe Cove 9 a.m. heading for Port Arthur. Wind started out about 20 mph out of SW and built up to about 30 mph. Just outside of Port Arthur breakwater, a squall came up with gusts up to 55 mph. Motor would not start. Finally, after installing new plugs, got it started. [It had to be nerve wracking to be in engine compartment in that type of squall and wind.] Inside Port Arthur [Canadian shore NW of Isle Royale] breakwater lost a batten taking down the main and circled several times to recover it. [A batten—*BAT-on*—is a long thin flat strip of wood that slides into a "slot" along the outside edge of a sail and helps to keep the sail taunt.] We approached a likely looking mooring which turned out to be the public marina. Two hundred yards before arriving, the motor developed a loud noise. Rain was coming down like everything and stung the face. We limped into a mooring 2 p.m. and discovered after man-handling the motor out and into a pickup, that the crank shaft was broken. We could not get parts or a new motor shipped in time, so we decided to leave on Sept. 15 without a motor.

Sept. 15, 1966

"Left with a light breeze and made about four or five miles along Ft. William water front when we became becalmed. Decided to try

Jarvis Bay to Windigo

towing the boat with our 3 hp dingy. Found we could make about 3 mph in a flat sea towing. A dark strip ahead forewarned us of an approaching stiff wind so we trailed the dingy and started off with Genoa jib up toward Flatland Island. Soon we had to use the working jib, as the wind built up to about 30 mph on a reach. [A *reach* is when the wind comes at 90° angle to boat—very fast for sailing.] We decided we could not get all the way to Washington Harbor on Isle Royale before dark, so anchored at the very end (SW) of Jarvis Bay. Good holding ground in 9 ft. of water.

Sept. 16, 1966

"Left Jarvis Island at 6 a.m. and just cleared the channel at the north end of Spar Island when our wind slacked off to near nothing. We towed by dingy for over an hour and finally got a bit of breeze. Going was so slow we abandoned the idea of going all the way to Portage Canal. Sailed with a light breeze behind us right up to the dock at Windigo. Cleared customs and started a long cocktail hour about 4 p.m.

Sept. 17, 1966

"Left Windigo by towing with the dingy at 6:40. A bit of a breeze turned up so we turned to go into Grace Harbor. The wind gave the boat such an acceleration after turning that *Lorelei* ran down the dingy before we could disconnect the tow line. *Lorelei* pulled the dingy around backwards. Clarke grabbed the rail and got on board but the dingy was swamped and got upside down. Quite an effective sea anchor. We threw out the anchor. Took down the main and managed to right and bail the dingy. Took the motor plugs out and dried it out. Finally got it running and towed Lorelei about 3 miles before any air came up."

There were no more entries about this trip and its disasters, but the crew and *Lorelei* obviously made it back home safely. Reading about this trip years later, I was left wondering how other sail-only ships had managed years ago, and what the steam ships later did when engines broke down and they had no "backup." The courage of captains and sailors of old will forever leave me in awe of them.

In the summer of 1967, we made a lengthy trip all the way to Sault St. Marie, through the locks, and into Lake Huron to Mackinac Island. We had good sailing and no problems the entire trip. *Lorelei*, while it seemed to me to be a fairly large boat, was a mere cork in a bathtub inside a lock that can also accommodate ore freighters! While I enjoyed that trip, I had grown to an age where I had other interests—especially a boyfriend, and not one who could come along on cruises as my sister Kathy's fiancé had. My only communication with that boyfriend in the pre-cell phone, pre-internet era was by pay-phone with a *lot* of nickels, dimes, and quarters—deposit sixty cents for the next three minutes, please. Pining for him (and he broke up with me a few months later) made me less attentive to the details of what I would later consider a unique experience, but that is the way of teens in every era of humanity.

Lorelei needed at least three people to man her. Once I graduated from high school in 1969, the last of my siblings, my parents found it harder and harder to find friends to sail with them. They made the decision to sell her and buy a "stink pot" converted trawler that the two of them could handle. I have no idea who bought her, or where she went after that. Now in my own senior years, I can't help but think back to those days on the "Big Lake" and the life lessons about work and cooperation I learned as crew on *Lorelei*, and especially the knowledge that there are forces in nature over which I have no control and only a great faith in a Power beyond myself will bring me home to a safe shore.

Deborah K. Frontiera grew up in Michigan's Upper Peninsula, has lived in Houston, TX, since 1985, and taught in Houston public schools until 2008. Now a "migratory creature," she spends the summer months in her beloved U.P. and the balance of the year in Texas. She has published fiction, nonfiction, poetry, and children's books, and edits the newsletter for the Upper Peninsula Publishers and Authors Association (UPPAA). She has helped judge many writing contests for students and adults. For details about her many books and accomplishments, visit her website: www.authorsden.com/deborahkfrontiera

The Typewriter

by Elizabeth Fust

It is imposing. Black. Old. Mysterious. Your hands tap out a quick sentence, "It was a dark and stormy morning," for indeed, outside of the decrepit antique shop, a storm rages. The letters tap out crisply, sternly, a polished defined black. You have to have the typewriter.

It sits perfectly at home on your roll-top desk. It commands the room. You spend some time staring at it, and then, forgetting work, food, sleep, and responsibilities, you spend all night at the keys until the tapping has become your favorite melody.

At first, the ink-impressed pages are only yours to see. But such ink is not meant for only one. You forget to put the papers away. At least, you think you must have forgotten; otherwise, how else were they laid out for your unexpected guest to find the next day?

The guest finds the words entrancing, mesmerizing. They declare you must find some outlet to publish the story you have written.

You postpone this step as you covet the stories as your own for only you to enjoy, but of course, you inevitably progress to submission. You craft perfect queries from the cold iron keys.

Applause. Adoration. They want more. So do you.

You go days without sleep. Food and drink become afterthoughts. Words pour like blood from a wound onto that wonderful bandage of paper. You don't know how you come up with it. You are much cleverer than you had previously thought yourself. And now? Now you are receiving the recognition you deserve.

It is almost too easy, you begin to realize. You blackout at your desk, and when you come to, there are pages and pages of neatly typed words. You wonder how you do it. Were you always this...gifted? You feel so tired and you just want to rest, but sleep doesn't come easily.

One day, you finally slip into a dreamless sleep. A noise breaks through your slumber. There is no one there. Odd. But the desk light is on. Did you leave it on? Yes, you are certain you did. But as you go to turn the lamp off, you are startled. There are words on the page. Words you did not write. Words wiser and more attractive by far than any you have ever written. And so it goes.

Every night after slaving away at the keys, you fall into a deep repose, your dreams chased by clacking. And when you awake, words fill the pages. Are you writing in your sleep? Going insane? You share the words, nevertheless.

People love the narratives; they crave them. The more you write and share, the more crazed the readers become. They need more. They follow you, stare at you, find where you live. They beg you for more. No, they demand it.

You are scared now. Terrified. You sleep more and more, but you become only more exhausted. You remember to eat and drink now, but your throat refuses to let you swallow.

You sit at the typewriter and type:
"What happened to me?"

And cupping your head in your hands you hear the keys clack and you see them moving of their own will as the ink presses out:
"—I have."

Special News Bulletin
— Famed Author Found Strangled

Early this morning a famed author was found unconscious and has been taken into intensive care. Police speculate that an intruder broke in and attempted to strangle the author with the ink ribbon of a typewriter found destroyed at the scene. The levers and keys of the demolished typewriter were found scattered around the body of the author. Reports from the scene state the author's hands were covered in blood and ink. There has been no update on the condition of the author, the acclaimed writer of several volumes. Several benefactors have offered to repair the typewriter as an act of good will in hopes of a recovery so the ardent fans may have more books from the author's beloved typewriter.

Elizabeth Fust is a senior English writing major and communication studies minor at Northern Michigan University who will graduate in Spring 2018. While at NMU, Elizabeth has worked as the student programming assistant at the Beamier U.P. Heritage Center, acted as an editor/web editor for *The Ore Ink Review* online literary journal, and participated in the NMU honors program and other campus groups. Her short story, "An Abandoned Dream," was published in the *U.F. Reader Issue #1*.

Minié Ball

by Giles Elderkin

Late in the afternoon of May 6, 1864, I took a single step back. While rotating to speak to Lt. Stritch, a .69 caliber rebel Minié ball whirred through the fringes of my beard and struck his chest with a sickening thwack. Stritch crumpled to the ground, unable to breathe.

For three years, I had witnessed battlefield deaths: some quick and clean as a sharpened scythe harvesting ripe grain, but most labored, struggling for last breaths, bloody bubbles forming through pursed lips. Stritch would not have an easy death, unless a lucky fragment of the bullet or the chest bones it surely broke happened to sever an artery. I dropped to my knees to try to make his last moments restful. His eyelids fluttered, and he tried to raise himself.

I supported his head in the crook of one arm and slung my canteen off my shoulder to give him a sip. He pushed aside the proffered water and slipped his right hand into his sack coat as some men do to confirm the bloody damage. The creases in his brow smoothed; his lips moved from a shocked "oh" into a serene smile. From the inner pocket of his coat he removed a miniature Bible containing an embedded lead slug.

Alternately kissing the book and the ball, he struggled to his feet. I tried to lead him to safety—we were in the midst of action on what would be known as the second day of the Battle of the Wilderness—but he shook me off. Raising both arms high above his head, he screamed to the heavens, "The Lord is my savior. I shall not want." The ululation of a rebel yell announced imminent attack, bringing us from the contemplation of heaven to the present hell.

We survived three more attacks before the darkness of a new moon prevented any action more significant than the skirmishing of picket lines. I fell asleep to the anguished cries of the wounded and woke the next morning to Stritch proclaiming the miracle of his survival to all in camp who listened and harangued all chance encounters we met during our unit's forced march that day to Spotsylvania.

Marching through a muddy crossroads, all eyes turned left to avoid staring at hundreds of bodies stacked like so much cordwood in front of the skeletal remains of a tavern. Even in my dotage fifty years later, the faintest whiff of decomposition transports me to the heat and stench of that accumulated carnage.

The chaplain fell out of line to give the dead a final blessing before their mass burial, and the column shuffled to a halt while the chaplain mumbled words only the dead could hear. Storming back after his prayer, the chaplain grabbed Stritch by the shoulder and spun him to face the bodies. "Lieutenant," he shouted, "those men care nothing for your miracle. Pray for your own understanding of why God granted you this great gift."

His words sliced into me with the power of a bayonet thrust. Although I did not feel Stritch's need to tell others, I held the burden of knowing that without my own chance turning, Stritch's Minié ball would have killed me. The chaplain forced me to address my own understanding of why the Lord chose me to live and let hundreds of thousands of others die in this monumental failure we call the Civil War.

•••

By the war's conclusion, Lt. Stritch had become Lt. Colonel Stritch, brevetted three times for extraordinary courage and bravery under fire. Before and after every battle, he kissed the Minié ball, proclaiming, "each man has only one fatal bullet with his name on it, and the Lord has saved me from mine."

That slug bore my name as well as his, but Stritch would hear nothing of my suggestion that his logic was flawed since a bullet could not be both fatal and nonfatal. Stritch came to understand God's purpose in his miracle. The lead had progressed through the Old Testament into the New and stopped at Matthew 6:13. Stritch believed the verse, "And lead us not into temptation, but deliver us from evil:" was his call to ministry to deliver mankind from the evil of this world.

I continued to struggle to understand my own survival, but Stritch was sure he knew the reason: my turning away from the bullet had allowed God to demonstrate His mission for Stritch. I was clearly midwife to his ministry.

After the war, Stritch matriculated at Princeton where he was ordained a Presbyterian minister. I returned to my Michigan home, married the banker's only child, and raised pigs, corn, and, eventually, six children. Stritch discovered the church I belonged to was looking to fill its pulpit and reminded me of my midwifery to his ministry. I felt compelled to use my influence as an Elder of our church and son-in-law to the banker who controlled the church's funding to convince our congregation to call Stritch to our pulpit.

In recognition of his education and wartime service, Stritch was titled "Reverend Colonel." His opening address promised we would become the new Eden where people sinned no more and snakes feared to slither. Behind his back, the community soon called him Moses, and like the Jews in their exodus from Egypt, there was much murmuring.

I realized too late that college had reformed him from a humble man who believed he was shielded by God from Rebel bullets to a religious prig. His sermons became long-winded and heavy on fire and brimstone. To hope for salvation, Stritch preached, "Each person must repent even the smallest transgression." Shortly before the end of every sermon, Stritch thumped his "preachin' Bible" on the pulpit one last time and removed the saving miniature book and Minié ball from his pocket. Waving the Bible in the air, he proclaimed, "Praise God's unknowable ways," and then kissed the projectile. The congregation provided an enthusiastic "Amen!"

Stritch smiled pleasure with the accolade for his message, misinterpreting what was for many only praise that one more Sunday message had concluded.

You may consider me cynical for saying this, but when times are good, people tend to favor the New Testament's kind and loving God. Stritch's angry, judgmental God played better during times of trouble. Unfortunately for Stritch, prosperity reined for several years after the war's conclusion. First in a trickle and then in a torrent, parishioners abandoned our congregation for the Universalist Church across the square, with their *We're all in this together, Brothers and Sisters* approach to salvation.

I would have joined the Universalists, but I was unwilling to break my family's ties to the Presbyterian church—my father-in-law was the head Elder—and I felt responsible to Stritch. Even after my father-in-law passed away, I kept my counsel and contributed more each year to keep the congregation solvent and the other Elders pacified.

During the summer of 1873, Stritch's increasingly bitter denunciations of the evildoers in the congregation—including a Sunday he called me out by name for lusting after my neighbor's property—reached new depths. The Elders, six of us, bearded veterans all, met to address our loss of membership.

"I have a new understanding," one said, "why the Romans slew the original disciples. They couldn't stand the constant haranguing."

"Lord help me," another confessed. "Sometimes I do wish his pocket Bible had only included the New Testament." I was not sure whether that Elder meant he wished the Reverend Colonel would only preach from the New Testament or whether a thinner Bible would have let the Minié ball complete its task.

It was one against five, but through time and habit, I firmly believed God had saved me from that Minié ball to support Stritch. With the death of my father-in-law, I now was the richest man in the county. I bought Stritch one more year in the pulpit with my offer to fund replacing the roof and tuckpointing the brick.

I begged Stritch to moderate his message. His rejoinder never changed: "God's will be done."

Events triggered by the Panic of 1873 solved the church's membership woes and saved Stritch from expulsion. Farmers, most of whom now belonged to the Universalist congregation, were devastated by the contracting money supply and gold becoming the only accepted currency. Banks foreclosed on farms because farmers had no ready money for seed or mortgages. During this disaster, the Reverend Colonel Stritch trumpeted, "God is not pleased with disbelievers in original sin." Pointing at the Universalist Church across the square he roared, "They now reap what they have sowed."

By the depression's end six years later, the Universalist Church stood empty, their pews sold to a congregation in Detroit. We Presbyterians doubled our sanctuary size to accommodate the chastened. Even the snakes in the fields hid at Stritch's approach. But all was not well with my pastor.

By 1880's Holy Week, I could no longer ignore the decline of Stritch's physical energy. He resorted to mid-afternoon naps. He confessed he had trouble sleeping, suffered constant headaches, and could not concentrate while writing sermons.

A year of stomachaches and consequent loss of appetite enervated his body. When he could choke down a meal, he felt nauseous and constipated. He celebrated his thirty-ninth birthday in the Sunday pulpit, going at us sinners hammer and tong.

In mid-sentence, he collapsed.

Once I had him home, I forced him to consider himself in a full-length mirror. Looking back at us was the visage of an emaciated prophet: Hair and beard prematurely gray. Eyes red and wild. Fingers twitching with palsy. Only his stentorian voice remained from his younger self.

"Have you considered what you are doing to anger the Lord?" I asked.

Stritch insisted he was a modern Job, being tested by God for greater things.

I chose not to suggest that the only thing he had lost was his health. I tried to use his hope of doing important work against him, arguing he couldn't do God's will if he were dead. "Why not?" he said. "Look at all Jesus accomplished after His death."

•••

Eventually, he agreed for me to pay for his admittance to a water cure in Battle Creek. The doctors subjected him to cold baths, tasteless whole grain foods, daily exercise, and a ban on cigars. I received weekly reports and was disturbed to read that during sleepless nights he conducted whispered conversations with God while clutching his saving Bible in one hand and holding the diminished remains of the Minié ball to his lips.

It took a year for the water cure doctors to admit defeat. With Stritch's mind and body now wasted, I brought him to a sanitarium for the insane in Detroit. The chief physician examined Stritch and concluded the case was hopeless. At the news, Stritch silently clenched and unclenched his hands. The doctor pried them open and retrieved the now tattered pocket Bible and the Minié ball, worn down to half its original size. He asked the meaning of these talismans.

I related our roles in Stritch's miracle at the 1864 Wilderness battle. "That's the Minié ball and the miniature Bible."

The chief physician held the projectile to the light. "The ball has done its work," he said.

"Sir," I said, "I do not understand your meaning."

"Every time your Reverend Colonel praised the Lord and kissed the bullet, a little lead leached from the slug into his body. He's dying from lead poisoning."

"So Stritch was right," I said. "That ball *was* his, *not* mine."

Giles Elderkin writes stories set in the distant past or in the not-so-distant future. He is the doppelganger of James M. Jackson, the award-winning author of the Seamus McCree novels, which include two set in Michigan's Upper Peninsula (*Cabin Fever* & *Empty Promises*). He splits his time between the remote U.P. woods and the low country of Georgia. You can find more information about him at https://gileselderkin.com/ or https://jamesmjackson.com/

Please Pass the Wisdom

by Jan Stafford Kellis

Life proved more difficult than I'd anticipated. I was nineteen, and by early August 1989, I'd given birth, moved across town, and been promoted at work all within my two weeks' (yes, two *weeks*) maternity leave. Under normal circumstances, a promotion would have been welcome, but arriving on the heels of my first-born, the new job presented a staggering challenge. I had yet to adapt to the magnitude of minutiae baby maintenance required and I was simply too exhausted to unpack at our new place. We scuttled between towers of boxes for several weeks, like dazed shoppers trolling store aisles, never realizing we were in the wrong store the whole time.

Ed, my live-in boyfriend, worked the swing shift in a plastics factory and was disinclined toward childrearing. His latest escapade had culminated in wrecking my car three weeks before our daughter was born, and transporting the baby to the sitter and myself to work presented an unwelcome complication. On work days, Ed tumbled out of bed at the last minute and ran out the door in a stained T-shirt, baseball cap on backwards, shoes untied, and slid into his friend's muffler-less car.

My mornings began at least three hours prior to punching the clock, wishing I could've punched something else, but knowing I didn't possess the energy. The credit union, where I worked, required professional attire—skirt, blazer, pumps, accessories. I quickly learned to don my blaz-

er *after* depositing the baby at the sitter's to hide the inevitable last-minute shoulder drools.

The new baby slept regularly—all day long, while I worked. I spent many nights cranking her mechanical swing every twenty minutes, letting it rock her to sleep, while I collapsed on the floor beneath the swing until her cries signaled me to sit up and turn the handle again. I frequently slept through my lunch break, shutting my new office door to lay my head on the desk. The pregnancy weight (and more) melted away quickly and effortlessly, resulting in my new drawn expression, complete with sunken cheeks. My zombie-esque state hampered my ability to learn my new position and decorated my face with dark bruises beneath my eyes.

I became preoccupied with sleep. If the devil himself had offered to relieve me for a few nights, I would have gladly surrendered my soul and reveled in the responsibility-free time, sleeping like the proverbial baby. Such fantasies, however captivating, were unlikely. My only recourse was to cope, exuding sunshine and diminishing the difficulties of single motherhood.

Coping is a family tradition. The only acceptable emotion in our stoic household when I was growing up was benign pleasantness; one was expected to camouflage any discomfort, infirmity, or inadequacy by maintaining a bright smile and an enthusiastic attitude. Not too enthusiastic, however: no jumping or shouting or pumping one's fist in the air If someone commented on one's ap-

Hiawatha Mine - Iron River

pearance, whether they said, "You look nice today" or "Your hair is on fire," the proper response never varied: "Thank you for letting me know." Running to the fire extinguisher, while this may be one's first inclination, would indicate panic. Panic was not on the list of allowed emotions. Employing the fire extinguisher with a calm authority, saving all of the hair and avoiding the indignity of a burned scalp, would have been the only acceptable course of action.

So I coped. I grinned until my face hurt and my teeth dried out and my lips stuck to them and people wondered if I battled an obscure, incurable smiling compulsion. I merrily phoned my friends and coworkers, begging rides to work, requesting a detour past the babysitter's, as if this were just another fun facet of new motherhood and living on my own. At a naïve nineteen, my actions illustrated my life philosophy: the old cliché about lying in the bed one has made. My bed was messy and inconvenient, difficult, and sometimes embarrassing, and I resented the situation and the actions I'd taken to create it. And yet, I coped.

Despite the adult-like trappings of my life—the baby, the career, the house, the live-in baby-daddy, the budget, the wardrobe—I didn't feel grown up. Grownups conducted themselves with poise and grace. They had real hairstyles and wore pristine pantyhose, while mine sported nail polish repairs on the legs and knots under my toes to hide the runs and snags. Grownups belonged to a secret society in which everyone always knew right from wrong, wore their confidence like a cashmere shawl, and effortlessly maintained their dignity. Grownups didn't merely cope—they possessed wisdom.

Dialing the sitter from work one day, I suddenly realized the need to identify myself. The sitter watched several children and, previously, I had only called her to discuss rates and hours, when I could use phrases like "the baby" or simply "Danielle." Now we were established clients, I couldn't very well say, "I'm calling about Danielle," without explaining who I was. The sitter couldn't give information to any old lunatic calling about one of her charges.

I mentally scrolled through several alternatives before uttering, "This is Jan,—uh, well—Danielle's mother." I gasped on the last syllable, nearly choking, my ears ringing. Spots obscured my vision.

"Yes, Jan. What can I do for you?" The babysitter, calm and assured, clearly a grownup, had already adjusted to the idea of my being someone's mother.

"Just a moment, please," I stammered. The shock of my pronouncement, "This is Danielle's mother," triggered a nervous reaction, probably classifiable as a panic attack, as the understanding landed on me like a full-body lead apron, dulling my senses and temporarily insulating me from reality. My hands shook; my voice wavered. A thin layer of sweat formed on my numb upper lip. Eventually, I recovered and completed the phone call, most likely speaking gibberish and causing the sitter to question my mental capacity. Invoking my inherent near-militant control, I slowly regained my composure.

The chaos in my brain gradually settled enough for one concept to surface: I was an adult, responsible not only for myself but also for another human being. Someone had not checked my ticket—they'd let me through the turnstile of adulthood without verifying my credentials. My first clear thought was: *There must be some mistake—I'm not yet finished being a child.* And then: *Wait! I haven't gained the wisdom yet!* Somehow I had skipped the Wisdom Acquisition Process through which every adult passes. I'd missed the seminar and there were no Cliff Notes. Initiated without my knowledge or consent, I'd been pitched rudely into the adult arena with a crying, sleepless baby and a non-attentive partner. Although, I reminded myself, I had made my bed. I was lying in it. I was coping.

How many other adults experienced and compensated for this lack of wisdom? Did all teenaged parents likewise suffer? Was I *really* someone's mother?

Nearly three decades have now passed, dissipating the desperation. At some point during those twenty-plus years, I realized I could leave the bed I'd made and adopt a new adage: "It's never too late to change direction." While not as catchy, realizing I had the power to correct my own course has served me well.

I have two daughters now, to both of whom I taught formal table manners, telephone etiquette, and how to make a bed with hospital corners. Although I was unable to endow them with erudition, somehow they acquired it without my help and they turned out fine. Better than fine, they possess a high level of wisdom and grace, evidenced by frequent eye-rolling and derisive comments. They are clearly wiser than I am.

All the time spent fretting over poor choices and messy beds—the interminable search for elusive perspicacity and confidence—comprised my self-education. Adopting a new cliché in my late twenties forced me to reflect on the past and seize my place in the land of grownups. While I will never attain the poise, grace, and dignity real adults possess, at least I know how to cope and can present a brave face to the world. I now know a formal Wisdom Acquisition Process doesn't exist—some people possess a natural self-assurance, masquerading as wisdom, probably present at birth and developed with age. I was not blessed with such grace, but I can manage.

So here I sit, an accidental grownup, reminiscing about my shaky ascension to adulthood, startling myself with recollections over twenty (or thirty) years old. My wrinkles present tangible evidence of experience while the wisdom remains stubbornly and conspicuously absent.

I watch my daughter with her own two daughters now, and she seems to possess a certain acumen for childrearing, an envious sense of confidence. It must have skipped a generation.

What's that? My hair's on fire? Please pass the fire extinguisher.

Jan Stafford Kellis is the author of the *Bookworms Anonymous* series, *Superior Sacrifices*, and *The Sunshine Room*. She lives in the eastern end of the U.P. where the inspiration is plentiful. When she's not reading or writing, she's probably visiting her daughters or her sister, or sewing, quilting, knitting, traveling, marathon shopping, or luxury camping. She hasn't been bored since 1974, when she first learned how to read.

One Shot Alice

by Sharon Kennedy

Once Alice learned to load the shotgun, there was no stopping her. Never before had she contemplated killing Jerk. Although she had long thought about his death, she hoped it would be a quick one while he still had a job and she was the sole beneficiary on his life insurance policy. All hope of that was gone now because Jerk had quit his job and there was no longer a policy so there was no longer any reason to keep him alive.

The hatred Alice felt for Jerk had grown over the years and he had nurtured it. Unwittingly, of course, because Jerk was stupid. She thought of ways to pick him off. It would have to be done outside and during daylight, and it would have to appear as an accident. Alice made sure folks knew Jerk was teaching her how to shoot. She was tired of calling him at midnight and asking him to come over and shoot the four-legged creatures that prowled around her place. Porcupines were her main concern. They chewed her porch steps with all the gusto of a kid chewing beef jerky.

Jerk's shotgun was old and heavy. The barrel wobbled when Alice aimed. She made sure people knew she wasn't a good shot—that she often missed her target. She showed a few friends her back porch where she had blown a hole through her basement window when she missed a porcupine gnawing on the bottom step.

Alice reasoned that you had to plan these things. You just couldn't phone your neighbor and say you had shot Jerk by mistake. No, that wouldn't do. The killing had to be well planned, but not too well planned. Just enough to be believable when the sheriff came around. You had to have allies. She'd learned that lesson at a young age. It was the only life lesson she never forgot. You had to have allies if you were to survive.

It was almost midnight when Alice turned off the lights and went to bed. She couldn't sleep. She wasn't thinking about the shooting, just how things never go as planned. Jerk was lucky, had always been lucky. Always came out smelling like a rose no matter how much heartache or abuse he heaped on others. Alice hated him for that. Hated him for saying he was blessed by God, for she knew his god was the evil one, not the God of Abraham and Jacob, but the god of Lucifer. How else could his luck be explained? He was a loser. A user. A psychopath. No loving godhead would bless such a monster, at least Alice didn't think so.

She dozed off and awakened at three. Every night it was the same. Three o'clock rolled around and Alice awoke. It didn't matter if she had been asleep for five hours or five minutes. She heard a noise on the back steps. Another porcupine chewing on her porch? A bear tearing apart her trash can? An intruder trying to break in? She was groggy when she reached for the shotgun. Cautiously, she opened the door. Jerk was standing there, drunk as a skunk, and wearing the hideous smile she had come to recognize as a prelude to abuse. It was too late to stop the trigger.

A feeling of relief ran through her as she watched him fall backwards. When his head hit the cement, he groaned. Alice knew she should phone 911 or a neighbor or just yell into the night, but she merely stood still and listened. The night was calm. No breeze stirred the leaves. No owls called to one another. As the moon came around the corner of her house, light fell across Jerk's face. It was twisted in agony.

Good, she thought. *Take a long time to die. Take twenty years. That's what you took from me. Two decades of my life that I'll never get back.* Alice had endured twenty years of verbal, emotional, and sexual abuse because she was too ashamed to admit it was happening. Nobody would have believed her anyway because everybody loved Jerk. Everybody that is except those closest to him. He groaned again. Alice looked at him one

more time before she closed the door and returned to bed.

The case was quickly closed. Not even manslaughter. After all, who would have expected a sweetheart lurking around your place at 3:00 a.m.? Porcupines, maybe, but not the man who loved you. From that night on, Alice slept peacefully until dawn. There was no reason to be on the alert. She had shot the monster who hunted her. Life was good.

Saturday Mornings on Chestnut Street

by Sharon Kennedy

Every Saturday morning from April through October, Virgil Blow cuts his grass. He owns a small house and three empty lots, and his John Deere purrs around and around until it runs out of gas or Virgil collapses. It's not unusual to see the ambulance turning into his driveway. The first time it happened, concerned neighbors rushed over to see what was wrong and offer assistance. Now they just ignore the commotion and within a few hours Virgil's wife brings him home none the worse for wear. One of their good-hearted neighbors invites them to a backyard barbeque. Mrs. Blow never worries about cooking Saturday dinner after spending most of the afternoon in the waiting room of the hospital, and someone always finishes cutting Virgil's grass.

Chestnut Street is a friendly, happy place in Salem, Illinois. There's a diverse mix of cultures, ages, races, and religions and everyone gets along. Greeks and Italians and Irish and Germans and Arabs and Indians and mongrels are all thrown together. Most of the men work at the local corn plant where

they run enormous machines that shuck, wash, cut, and can tons of fresh corn.

In the winter, the fellows draw unemployment, watch television, and take an occasional weekend trip to Michigan where they ice fish. Their wives are teachers or hairdressers or waitresses. The kids go to the local schools, and every Friday night they play football or basketball. When there's no game, they rollerskate at the rink while their parents watch. When the rink closes, kids and parents pile into cars and head for the Dairy Queen on South Broadway. There's never any trouble— no drugs, no alcohol, no truancy. If it weren't for the person residing at 1947 Chestnut, the street would be utopia. But no street is perfect. There's always a Chester Cunningham to upset the apple cart.

Chester moved into 1947 Chestnut Street in 1974. For years, everyone thought he was normal. He worked at the corn plant like the other men. He cut his grass on Saturday mornings. In good weather, he read the Sunday paper on his front porch while he drank Nescafe from a huge coffee mug that read "Pa, yer coffee's ready." He purchased the mug from the Salvation Army store on Main Street where he made most of his purchases. It wasn't unusual for the men of Salem to recognize one of their shirts or jackets on his back, or a pair of gray flannel trousers on his legs. His neighbors' belts encircled his waist, their ties hung around his neck, and their hats perched on his head. After a while, Chester didn't have to drive to the Red Shield Store and pay for his purchases. People merely dropped boxes of clothing and household goods on Chester's doorstep or hauled junk behind his house. He thanked all the kind people and everyone was happy.

One morning, he stopped showing up at the corn plant. He didn't bother to call in sick or inform management he was quitting. After twenty-five years, he simply never went back to work. He ignored letters the company sent him, and he didn't answer the telephone. He refused to open his front door when Corn King sent a manager out to hear his story. Eventually he filled out the necessary forms and his Social Security check arrived every month along with the dividends from his investments.

When neighbors knocked on his doors, Chester ignored them. Their well-meaning cards and notes went unopened and unanswered. He left the phone off the hook to avoid inquisitive callers. Eventually, he wrote a letter to Southwestern Bell and requested his phone be disconnected. When an old friend cupped his face and peered into Chester's living room, he popped up at the window and scared him. Over the years, almost everyone in the neighborhood had given Chester a variety of Halloween masks, and he delighted in using them whenever the urge struck. He hadn't taken a dislike to his old friends and neighbors. He just couldn't be bothered with them and their meaningless chatter about the weather or the St. Louis Cardinals or who bowled a perfect game at the town's only bowling alley.

Chester was no longer bound by a certain date on the calendar. For him, every day was Halloween or Christmas or Easter or Flag Day or somebody's birthday. He was sixty years old, still a young man by the nation's standards, and he answered to no one. As far as everyone knew, he had no nagging wife, no whining adult children, and no nosy relatives to hound him. He didn't bother anyone and, had it not been for the grass situation, the relationship between him and his neighbors would have dissolved into nothing but complacent acceptance.

Once Chester no longer worked at the plant, he had lots of time to amuse himself. Unwittingly, his neighbors had sparked his hobby by giving him hundreds of junk items, which in his opinion, were perfect for a variety of art projects. Along with pounds and pounds of clothing, there was a good assortment of cracked dishes and broken pottery and mismatched flatware, all hungry for resurrection. There were sacks of rusty metal tools and Eight O'Clock Coffee cans filled with thousands of rusty bolts and nuts and nails—some bent, some perfect. There were thirteen old snares, one with the skeleton paw of a small animal still in it, either a rabbit or raccoon or mink, left behind when the tortured animal chewed off its paw and wandered back into the woods to die on its own terms.

There were bits and pieces of leather from belts or harnesses or handbags. There were hoes and rakes, old engines and come-alongs, broken lathes and handsaws, hammers with no heads, chipped axes, and bags, boxes and wooden washtubs teeming with bits-and-bobs of miscellaneous junk. Chester had a gold mine at his fingertips. His house and truck were paid for, his needs were few, and he had a nest egg the size of an ostrich egg. He was ready to begin his life's work. He was going to become an artist.

When Chester was young, he had worked at his grandfather's blacksmith shop. He loved being a smithy. To take a straight piece of iron and fire and bend and pound it into something beautiful was his heart's desire. He never again would work for another man. He was his own boss. He threw himself into his projects. His locked garage became his workshop, and when the fire in the forge burned low, Chester bellowed it back to life. Long into the night, the neighborhood echoed with the clang of his hammer as it forced a new creation into existence.

The months passed quickly, spring came early, and Chester forgot all about his grass.

By the end of April, it was eight inches high. Dandelions thrived. Broadleaf weeds, hidden for years, suddenly appeared bringing their relatives with them. Cracks in the driveway soon filled with blades of grass. His neighbors endured the dandelion plague. They sprayed and broadcast and weeded their yards. They trimmed and clipped and mowed. Up one side of Chestnut Street and down the other, spring had reared its lovely head. Rain fell on cue, and every night grass grew another inch while the residents slept away the hours.

By Memorial Day, Chester's grass was a foot high, and the timothy was higher. Neighbors pounded on his doors and taped notes to his windows. They complained to the city. In desperation, they gathered at Virgil Blow's house for a summit. They talked and planned and consulted a lawyer. They threatened. They pleaded, but Chester Cunningham was oblivious to everything. He heard nothing but the hiss and spit of hot iron as it hit the water pail. His every waking hour was consumed by iron, courtesy of the endless supply his neighbors had given him.

The morning of July 4 dawned bright and beautiful. Virgil Blow decided it was time to take matters into his own hands. After all, his great-grandpappy had homesteaded Salem. As part of the town's lineage, it was his responsibility to keep the neighborhood neat and tidy if the city wasn't going to do it for him. He added a little oil to his lawn mower and filled it with gas. Then he headed down the sidewalk to Chester's house. If nobody else would do the job, they could count on Virgil to get it done.

He wasn't sure the John Deere could tackle Chester's hayfield, but it was worth a try. He raised the blade to its highest setting and released the choke. The machine inched its way onto Chester's property. His next-door neighbor, the Widow Wirt, looked out her window and saw Virgil undertaking a monumental task. She mumbled a silent prayer that his heart wouldn't give out before the job was done, then she flung open her front door and cheered him on. "Go Virgil, go!" she yelled. "Give it all you've got." Of course he couldn't hear her voice above the noise of the mower, but she felt good that she had done her part to encourage if not physically abet Virgil.

The Deere balked, but didn't stall. Slowly, slowly Virgil cut a small swath. He kept two wheels on the sidewalk and two on the grass. On his second turn, he gave the Deere a little more gas and charged ahead. He needed a brush hog, but years ago when he had sold his farm and moved to town, he had paid some fellows to haul the hog to Chester's backyard. Virgil coaxed the Deere to keep working, and the machine was worthy of its name.

Back and forth, back and forth, Virgil kept a steady rhythm. He forgot about his aches and pains. He ignored the heat of the sun and his growing thirst. It took two hours, but he finished the job. He felt so good he moved on to the Widow Wirt's lawn, then to the next neighbor, and the next until he had mowed every yard and empty lot on Chestnut Street. He didn't collapse until he got home. Mrs. Blow called the ambulance, and the handsome young medics hooked Virgil up to an IV. Five hours later when he was released from the emergency room, he was feeling fine. The Widow Wirt, herself, provided the hot dogs for the night's barbeque where Virgil was hailed a hero.

Chester watched all the goings-on from a large hole in the green window shade of his dining room window. When he tired of watching his neighbors' merriment, he sat on a mended rocker in the middle of his living room and rocked himself into a corner. Not reclusive by nature, the many months of isolation had taken a toll on his nerves. A tiny pang of guilt shot through him, but he dismissed it as foolishness. What did he care if Virgil Blow had sunstroke? Chester didn't ask him to cut his grass. What did he care if the people on Chestnut Street thought him a bit odd? He was his own man, and if his daddy had taught him one thing it was to look out for himself. 'Course, daddy had died one summer night during a bar brawl and nobody found him for three days by which time it was too late to do anything except bury him, but that was beside the point. Chester's neighbors didn't want him to die. They just wanted him to cut his grass and give them the time of day. They wanted their pleasant, outgoing neighbor back.

Along about 9:30 in the evening, fireworks blasted from every corner of Salem, which got Chester's heart thumping and his dogs howling as if someone had hacked off their tails. Kids set off rockets outside his front door. Motorcycles raced across his driveway to the alley behind his house. The din outside matched the din inside his head. He rummaged through boxes of costumes until he found one that passed for Uncle Sam. When everything was in place, including a gray wig and beard, Chester flung open his front door and marched outside to the amazement of the crowd.

Virgil Blow was the first to greet him with a hardy handshake. Chester extended his hand and apologized for letting his grass grow so long and promised to keep it cut. He thanked Virgil for all the work he had done that morning. The astonished neighbors clapped and cheered and welcomed Chester back from the dead. Everyone was happy.

As he sat on his porch enjoying the Widow Wirt's fresh lemonade and orange cake, Chester remembered all the little items he had made. He went back in his house and returned with baskets and boxes full of forged candlesticks, horseshoes, ashtrays, picture frames, trivets, and toys. Toys for infants were made from rag clothing. Toys for older tots were forged from bits and pieces of scrap iron. Young and old alike gathered around, chose what they wanted, and praised Chester for his imaginative art pieces and his generosity. The evening continued on a high note with beautiful fireworks and plenty of nice words for everyone.

Chester felt happier than he had in a long time. Then an amazing idea struck him. He offered to teach blacksmithing to anyone interested in learning how to manipulate iron into something beautiful. When he made his announcement, the crowd issued a loud cheer.

Thereafter, life returned to normal for the folks on Chestnut Street. When Chester died a month later, the entire neighborhood mourned his passing. Then the women looted his house, taking back as many of their former belongings as they could carry. After all, a dead man had no need for bits and pieces of everything that could be repurposed into something else.

About a month after the funeral, Chester's long-lost twin brother showed up and claimed 1947 Chestnut Street as his own. Everyone welcomed him. The men gave him a hardy handshake, and the women brought freshly baked bread or cookies still warm from the oven. Chet Cunningham thanked them all and informed them he was taking over his brother's business. He hoped the noise from his forge wouldn't bother them. He was assured it was no trouble, no trouble at all.

Virgil had been cutting his grass, but now that Chet was here, Virgil figured the task would fall to him. He mentioned that Chester had left a mighty fine mower in the garage. After a few weeks, the grass was getting quite long, and nobody knew what to do so they held another summit at Virgil's house. The Widow Wirt volunteered to approach her new neighbor and suggest he cut his grass.

Chet Cunningham opened the door by her third rap. He was covered in soot from head to toe. She recognized his clothes as those of her long dead husband's, his shoes as discarded moccasins from the Native American neighbor to her right, and the scarf wrapped around his head as once belonging to the only Moslem family in town. Her visit lasted only a minute.

She hurried home and called Virgil Blow. "Keep your John Deere well-oiled and gassed," she said. "The ghost of Chester has returned."

Sharon M. Kennedy is a newspaper columnist who lives alone on a quiet country road in Brimley, MI. She is the author of *Life in a Tin Can*. Her "tin can" is a 1968 Marlette mobile home still in pristine condition. Within the confines of this metal structure, she writes short stories and newspaper columns that amuse her readers with memories of the past and humorous observations on present-day life. One of her essays was recently accepted for publication in the *2018 Erma Bombeck Writers' Workshop Humor Anthology*. You can email Sharon at thetincanpress@gmail.com.

True Confessions of an Introverted, Highly-Sensitive Middle School Teacher

by Amy Klco

f you were to make a list of qualities you want for your child's teacher, chances are likely that somewhere in that list, you would have words like "caring," "sensitive," "compassionate," and perhaps even a phrase like "thinks about my child as a whole person." In fact, as a parent, you might consider someone like me as the perfect teacher for your child. I am very in-tune to the feelings of others. I am hyper-aware of negative feelings in my students—whether they be fear, anxiety, depression, or anger. When a student is upset, I can defuse the anger before it gets out of control. When a student is feeling anxious or scared, I can help them to slowly face their fears, at a pace that feels comfortable to them. And when a student is feeling sad or depressed, I will reach out to them, listen to them, and let them know that they are not alone in their struggles. Especially for parents of highly-sensitive children, this type of teacher might seem like a welcome relief.

Now, let me tell you why, instead of making me an ideal teacher, my sensitivity has actually been a huge disadvantage in this profession.

Before that, though, let me tell you a bit about why I went into teaching in the first place. Very often, people who go into teaching do so because they had a good experience in school. It makes sense—if you are good at something, you're more likely to want to keep doing it. The problem with this approach, however, is that it means you may have trouble understanding when a student is struggling.

On the other hand, my school experience was not a good one—I struggled in almost every way a kid can struggle. I struggled academically. It was very hard for me to learn to read and do basic math calculations, which translated in my mind as "being stupid." I struggled socially. I was an odd kid, quiet, and just plain different from other children. I was easy to pick on—and the other kids picked on me a lot. In addition to all of that, I was also struggling with depression, even from a young age. By the time I was in high school, this depression led to recurring suicidal thoughts. Many times, the focus of my school day was not on learning, but on fighting my own inner demons.

So if I had all these troubles in school, why would I want to go back there again? Why would I want to become a teacher and spend the rest of my life in this environment? The answer is simple—I wanted to help others. I wanted to be the kind of teacher I always wished I'd had.

I didn't realize, when I started out, how difficult that would be.

Okay, let's be clear. It's not as if I didn't know that becoming a teacher would put me outside my comfort zone. I knew I would have to learn to speak in front of people. I knew I would have to be able to control a class. I realized that most teachers tend to be extroverts (or at least introverts who can handle a lot of "people time.") I also believed—and still do—that students deserve to have all kinds of teachers and that our quiet, more sensitive students deserve to have role models in the school just as much as our louder kids do. I wanted to be that role model.

I like to think I have been that role model in my over thirteen years of teaching. However, this job has also taken its toll on me and honestly, I'm not sure how much more I can take. It is not the students, per se, that are wearing me out. More than anything, it is the stories they tell me, the things that they go through, and just how helpless I am to do anything about it.

One example of this is Tara. Tara was homeschooled for several years due to high anxiety levels. Even when she did return to public school, she had a very high rate of absenteeism. When she started middle school, she was far behind her peers in both reading and math. This may be because of a learning disability, it could be a result of her ADHD, or it might just be that she had "insufficient learning opportunities." The problem is this: We can't certify her as having a learning disability unless we can prove that she was provided with "ample opportunities to learn the material." And we can't do that if she is not in class. We need her to be in school before we can even prove that she needs special help with school.

As a teacher, I want to make sure she is here in school. After all, she can't learn if she's not here. Also, to be totally honest, if she doesn't learn, she won't do well on her standardized test, and the results of that test affect my evaluation. I try hard to make decisions based on what is best for the child, not on how it will affect their test scores—but that thought is always in the back of my mind. (I've had enough bad evaluations that it does make me worry.)

On the other hand, as someone who has been there, who has dealt with anxiety and depression, I feel for her. I know how hard it can be just to sit in class when you feel like you are falling apart inside.

I was happy to see her the first day of school the next year. She ran up to me, a huge smile on her face, to give me a big hug. She seemed very excited about the start of school. Which is why I was surprised when she wasn't at school the second day. By the third day, her absence didn't surprise me, but it did make me sad. I was worried about her—worried about how she was doing in the short run, and also worried about how her lack of attendance would affect her in the long run.

I was relieved, then, when the social worker came to tell me that she had come to school on the fourth day, after the principal had called her house. She had talked with the social worker for almost an hour and now needed a place to take a break for a bit before going to class. She had asked to come see me. As it worked out, it was during my prep, so I was able to spend some time with her. I asked her if she wanted to talk, and then just closed my mouth and listened.

The stories she told me broke my heart. She told me about dealing with anxiety and depression. About not being able to sleep at night because of worry and about not being able to come to school the next day because she hadn't slept, about how she's been cutting, how she always wears long-sleeve shirts to hide the scars on her arm. And she told me about how, over the summer, she had actually attempted to kill herself. As a teacher, we usually want our students to be successful in what they do—this is one time I was relieved to hear that she had failed in her attempt.

The hardest thing was that these stories were not new to me. I've heard them before, from other students, from those close to me, from myself. I've lived through having a student kill himself—from the first day, finding out just before all the students did, to the day of the funeral. I don't ever want to go through that again.

And so, I take the time to listen to my students. If I need to report it, I will (I tell the kids right up front that if I am "afraid that they might hurt themselves or someone else," I have to report that to the administration.) In this case, the principal already knew. Her parent knew. She was already seeing a counselor. There was nothing I could do for her except the most important thing of all—listen.

Hotel Cadillac - St. Ignace

I let her stay in my classroom the rest of the day. I probably should have sent her on to her other classes after a "reasonable break time." In fact, my principal said as much to me later, implying that I had let this kid "sucker" me into letting her avoid class.

Maybe she's right. Maybe I should have been firmer with Tara, sent her off to class despite her anxiety, made her "suck it up and deal with it." Maybe Tara was taking advantage of my kindness—I'm sure there have been students in my career who have done this.

But here's the thing: I would rather be suckered by one hundred kids who are taking advantage of my kindness than have just one kid who really needed my support not get it.

I know what it's like to be hurting inside. I know how hard it can be to finally ask for help. I know the feeling of finally opening up to someone, asking for their support, and not getting it. But I also, thankfully, know the feeling of opening up to someone and having them really listen, having them really care and be there for you. Those caring people have saved my life more than once.

And so, I will continue to be the "too-nice" teacher. Let others judge me. Let them imply that I am not a good teacher. Maybe I will lose my job one day—maybe I'll get one too many bad evaluations because I am more concerned with my students' mental health than their test scores. Maybe I will have to leave teaching one day—perhaps soon—because I am just too burned out, too emotionally exhausted from being the one person who sees these kids hurting and actually takes the time to reach out to them. Maybe I should never have gone into teaching in the first place, when I so clearly have trouble with giving kids the "tough love" they require.

But maybe, just maybe, I have also helped to save a life. If so, then it has all been worth it.

Death Comes to Visit

by Amy Klco

"It won't be much longer. Come as soon as you can."

We got the text just minutes before I was going to leave for a business trip. My fiancé's dad, Ben, had been doing poorly. Earlier in the year, they discovered the tumor in his brain, a tumor that had apparently been there his whole life, like a ticking clock, just waiting for this moment. Now, it was growing, pushing out his ability to think clearly and destroying his body from the inside out.

I've always had a bit of a knack for premonitions. Not a lot, but the big things. I know if a baby will be a boy or a girl before they are born. And I often have a sense of when death it is coming. At this point, though, it didn't take a premonition to know Ben's time was soon. After his latest stroke, they had moved him to a nursing home. And now, it was just a matter of waiting for the inevitable.

So when we got the text, we knew what it meant—it was time to go see him before it was too late. My business trip was forgotten as we packed the car for a different type of journey. There were some things that were more important than work. And what was important to me was being there for my fiancé.

After a four-hour drive, we arrived at the nursing home about eleven o'clock at night. They still let us in. Their policy was that you could come visit your loved ones whenever you wanted. In a world where there are so many stories of elders being abused in homes like this, it was a good way to promote transparency. I think, also, they just wanted to encourage people to visit their loved ones on whatever schedule they could manage. Perhaps, too, they realized that sometimes the visit couldn't wait until morning.

Ben was lying in bed, thinner than last time we'd seen him, only about a month earlier. We'd been told that he had stopped eating over a week ago, so it wasn't a surprise. But it did bring home the message that it wouldn't be long, now. He looked, if you will forgive my analogy, like the pictures I've seen of holocaust victims. But in this case, the starvation had been his own choice. That is, if his mind was even capable of making choices at that point.

My fiancé pulled up a chair next to Ben's bed, held his hand, and tried to rouse him enough to let him know we were there. His eyes opened and seemed to flicker with awareness—maybe. And then seemed to glaze over again. Was he awake? Was he conscious? It was impossible to tell. But my fiancé kept talking anyway. "Dad? Dad? Papa? I'm here. It's me, Paul."

I sat in a chair at the foot of his bed. I closed my eyes, closed off my sense of sight, and opened my mind to my sixth sense. Over the summer, I had learned how to perform Reiki. Reiki is, at its core, the idea that you can channel the healing light from the Universe and direct it toward someone in need. And when I was channeling Reiki, I could feel...something. I could see, with my mind's eye, the white light of Reiki energy coming into me, feel it circle my body, go into his, and circle back through mine again.

And when the energy came from his body into me, I could also sense his feelings. He knew we were there, he wanted to talk, to reach out to us, but it was so hard. His mind was so far away, buried so deep under skin, beneath his remaining muscles, even below his bones. He couldn't make this body of his respond any longer to the outside world. But under it all, deep within his mind, he was still there.

And what I felt most, beyond his inability to reach the outside, was his fear. He knew his time was near. Perhaps that's why he had stopped eating—it was time and he was willing his body to finish the process. And yet, he couldn't bring himself to let go. Because what would happen then?

He was, as Paul had told me, an avid atheist. There would be no sermons at his funeral, no prayers said over his grave. He had lived his whole life without believing that there was "something more" in life. But now, as he faced his death, his biggest fear was that he might have been right.

And then, just as his fear had come to me silently traveling on this path of energy between us, I got another message. Not from him. Not from me. From the Universe, itself. From God, if I can use that word. Not an old man with a long, white beard. He was—it was—a giant ball of light, of energy. Almost blinding within my shut eyelids. And the message God sent to me was one word: love.

Tears welled up in my eyes at the power of the word. And I knew at once the message I needed to send to Ben. I told him, over and over again in my mind, sent on this wave of light and energy, "You are loved. You are loved here on earth, by your family, by your friends. So many people love you here. But there is more. The Universe loves you. God loves you, more than you will ever know. More than you can ever understand."

"But I don't believe," Ben's fears came back to me. "But I've done things in my life. Hurt people. And I don't believe. How can he love me, when I don't believe in him?"

"He does love you. This love is..." I took a deep breath, soaking in the love I was feeling. It was almost too much. I felt like I would explode with the wonder of it all. "You are loved." I said at last, not even trying to describe the indescribable feeling. "You have always been loved and you will always be loved. And he's ready for you to come home now. It's okay. We'll be okay here. It's time for you to go home." Before we left, I said goodbye. He nodded and squeezed my hand.

If this were a novel, that would have been the moment when he closed his eyes forever. But real life is a bit more complex than that. He didn't pass away that night. We visited him again. Again, he was unresponsive. Except that he moved his hand. He reached for my hand and held it tight. And again, I heard his fears, and again I reassured him. "Yes, you are loved. You are loved here. We love you very much. But the Universe loves you even more. It's okay. All will be okay. It's time to let go of this world and go toward the love."

He passed, peacefully, early the next morning.

Amy Klco is a National Board Certified teacher with a BA in English and art, as well as three MAs in education. Her real passion, though, is in helping "tender-hearts"—those who feel a lot and often hurt a lot as a result. Her goal is to change the way society thinks about "tender-hearted" people. She wants tender-hearts to know they are not alone and that they have wonderful traits to share with the world, while at the same time helping the world understand how to help tender-hearts reach their amazing potential! Find out more at enchantmentpress.com.

On Turning Forty

by Jennifer Lammi

Forty lessons somewhat learned,
Each to a varying degree;
The lessons that I did not learn
Were never meant for me.

Forty paths not taken
Toward what will never be;
Each one led to forty more,
Then on to infinity.

Forty roads, some wide and fast,
Captured restless feet;
Some meandering and overgrown—
A place to rest, to eat.

Forty rivers, winding creeks,
Where every time I had to leap—
Dashing, flying, falling, crashing,
Sinking in the deep.

Forty valleys, mountain peaks,
Harsh passages across the sea—
Forty people I have hurt,
And forty have hurt me.

Forty years, like forty waves,
Washed treasures to the shore.
Should I? Could I? Might I dare
To ask for forty more?

Jennifer Lammi is a freelance writer whose poetry and personal essays focus on northern, small-town life, simple living, and connection with the natural world. She is a freelance writer and editor of the Marquette Regional History Center's quarterly journal, *Harlow's Wooden Man*. Born and raised in the Upper Peninsula, many generations of her ancestors have called the U.P. home. She lives in Marquette with her husband, two cats, and three dogs. She loves reading, exploring the U.P., and having bonfires with friends under the stars. Her writing can be found at www.smilingintothesun.com

"Yoopers"

by Raymond Luczak

"Have you heard the new word 'Yooper'?"

"'Yooper'? What the hell's that?" Grandma is pushing a rolling pin across a big ball of dough on the counter. She's done this a thousand times. I bet she could do it in her sleep. The transistor radio is playing Elton John's "Rocket Man," my favorite song of the moment, at a low volume.

"You know the U.P., right? You add e-r to the end of that, so it looks like U.P. er, and it sounds like Yooper."

"What's the point of that? We've always been here."

"No, no, Grandma. The Indians were here first."

"Well, I don't remember seeing them around much."

"That's because we drove them away."

"Good riddance."

"Grandma!"

"Well, it's true." She points to the dough. "You wanna learn how to make pasties or not?"

I stand closer to Grandma.

"Hey. Move back a bit."

"Sorry."

She folds the dough over a puddle of sifted flour and rolls the pin over it again. "It doesn't have to be thin like for pie. A little thick is nice. Keeps the filling hot. Good for you when you're cold and lots of snow outside."

She cuts the dough into four equal parts and rolls them until they all have the same round size.

"Grandma, I know. I've eaten your pasties many times." Today is a snow day for the schools in the area, but Grandma lives three houses down the street from where I live, so it wasn't a big deal to go climbing up on the mountainous snowbanks and walking along the ridge to her house. The snow's high enough that I could climb up atop her porch roof. I'm home for the weekend. I have two more years of college left to go at Northern Michigan.

Anyway, I'm hungry. She had me peel potatoes, rutabagas, and carrots, and cut them all up. She sliced the potatoes. She said that using carrots might offend a number of pasty purists. "If it tastes good, who cares what anyone thinks?" That's what she always says.

She sprinkles flour a bit more on the dough and goes for a great push. The dough looks thicker than a pie crust. She scoops out some lard.

"Grandma!"

"What?"

"You're using lard!"

"So?"

"Dad says he's not supposed to eat lard anymore."

"Whyever for?"

"It's bad for his heart."

"Says who?"

"His doctor."

She rolls her eyes. "A little lard's not gonna kill anyone." She continues spreading lard like butter. "There. Now, here, this is what you do. You break up that burger meat and spread it like you're making it for pizza."

I dig into the cold squelch of ground raw beef and break it apart until it looks like an anthill.

"That looks good. Now get me that green bowl." She points to a pale green ceramic bowl on a lower shelf in the pantry. It's big and heavy.

"Now, what you need to do, just put the potato and burger bits in there, toss in the onions, carrots, ruta, salt, and pepper. Stir it all up. Use your hands if you want."

I pour the chunky onion bits all around the beef. I pile carrot slices on top. It's strange to feel at first—the wet cold of beef against the shards of onion, but I come to like the sensation. The mixture of whites, pinks, and oranges make me think of Jell-O mold cakes for some reason. I shake the salt and pepper into the bowl.

"More, more," she says. "You want lots of spice, Molly."

I shake the salt and pepper even more. They start to look like candy sprinkles.

"That's enough. Now mix it all in."

I dive in and mush it and roll the mixture over and over like the way Grandma folds a chunk of dough over before pressing it down with her rolling pin.

"That looks good. Now we got to divide that up four ways for here, see?"

I nod and scoop as much as I can with my hands and let it fall into one of the four dough pieces.

"Now, now. You don't want all that to touch the edge, see? Just keep it all in a circle. Give it a bit of round the edge. Ja?"

I nod. I scrape the mixture back into the circle.

"Looks good. Now finish the other three." She is pulling out a baking sheet and unrolling some foil all over it. The kitchen is getting hotter from the woodstove. Grandma doesn't want to change over to an electric stove. Woodstoves are all she knows.

I try to distribute the amount of food evenly between the dough pieces.

She pushes more lard off the butter knife onto each pile.

"Okay, okay. You got to pull this up and over, and crimp it like this. See?" She sets down the knife and folds the dough to the side until it closes into half a circle. She pinches the edges and grabs a fork and presses its tines along the edges. "Do it like that. Nice and pretty."

As I pull up a flap of dough slowly and carefully, I feel afraid that it will tear off, but it doesn't. It stretches almost like rubber. I reach to the other side of the pasty and try to pinch its edge like how Grandma does it. The pasty looks bigger now that its dense filling is inside.

She hands me a fork. I feel like Grandma as I press along its edge.

"There you go. You can do the other two, then." She pulls up her apron and wipes the flour off her hands. She sips some coffee. "The radio said twenty-two inches today, ja?"

"Yeah."

"Not bad. I've seen worse. '38 was the worst. The snow was so high that you had to dig tunnels right there in downtown. Imagine that!"

"That would be so cool!"

She brings the baking sheet over to the counter. "Now, this is a bit tricky. Just you watch." She brushes all the flour away from the front of the pasties and holds the edge of the sheet just underneath the counter. She slides one pasty across the counter to the edge and tilts the sheet a little as the pasty is carried lovingly onto the sheet. "There!" She looks at me. "Your turn."

She holds the sheet as I push the next pasty onto the sheet.

"There you go!"

We both laugh.

"Now I want you to hold this."

I feel the weight of all four pasties on the sheet as she bends down and opens the oven. Its blast of heat hits us like an explosion.

"Just put it there." She points to the middle shelf.

I can't believe how iron-hot the oven is as I lean forward, afraid of dropping the pasties. But I do slide the sheet into the oven.

"Now we have to wait, oh, about an hour. Just have to keep an eye on it." She glances up at the clock on the wall.

"Okay."

"Now we have to clean up the kitchen." She hands me a wet rag. "Wipe away the flour." I wipe it twice to make sure that each bit of flour is indeed gone. I toss it into the hamper since Grandma has so many rags, usually cut up from Dad's worn-out shirts.

She hauls the ceramic bowl from the table to the sink, and fills it up with soapy water.

"Do you want to watch some TV while we wait?"

"Naw. I just want to watch the snow." The falling has gotten heavier since I arrived at Grandma's house. All that white looks so pretty.

She stops the water and wipes her hands again. She sits opposite me at the kitchen table. She lifts the gauzy curtain to look outside. "Sure looks pretty, but the plows...." She shakes her head.

I look at her. Her long white hair is woven into a bun with bobby pins. She is wearing a pale blue print with a white apron. The back of her hands and forearms are covered with liver spots. Her blue eyes have a bit of aqua green in them.

I wonder again about Grandpa. He died two years before I was born. He was supposed to be a quiet man, but if something irked him so, he could blow up real fast. That's what Mom always said.

"Tell me again about the Curry house." She used to be a cook for the most famous man in Ironwood. He was the first president of two new banks, and he had a fancy house built by the high school. He knew all of the important people in the early years of Ironwood. Then Grandma met Grandpa and got married and had two more kids after Mom. Her first husband died in a mining accident. She refuses to talk about him.

I love listening to Grandma's voice when she tells her stories about when Ironwood was young. I know them all by heart, but that doesn't matter. She is too happy to repeat herself. She rarely tells her stories in a chronological order; she often drifts off with tangential anecdotes until she returns to her starting point. So many people that she used to know are gone. She rarely goes to Mass because she has so much pain in her hips. As long as she doesn't have to use the stairs, she's okay.

I don't say a word as she speaks in such a way that I've never heard anyone speak. There is a hint of Swedish, and Finnish too. She knew so many immigrants who didn't know a word of English when they arrived in America, and she's probably taught them a number of things without realizing it.

I'm one-quarter Swedish, one-quarter Finnish, and one-half Polish. That's what I tell people when they ask where I come from.

Grandma suddenly notices the clock. "Grab a potholder and open the oven. I wanna see if it's ready."

I grab a dirty potholder that was made from a holey towel and pull down the hot handle.

There, in the blast of fire, the pasties are nicely browned.

"Hmm." She gets up and peers down into the oven. "Yes, they're ready." She pulls another potholder off its hook and hands it to me. "You can take them out."

I feel as if my bangs will catch fire as I lean down and lift the sheet of pasties out of the oven. "Where do I—?"

"There." She points to a wooden cutting board on the counter. "Put it there."

I slide the pasties off the sheet carefully. "Wow. They look so good."

She grips my shoulder. "That's because you helped me."

"So how many minutes do we have to wait?"

"Ten, fifteen minutes." Grandma returns to her chair.

"Okay." I set the table with a pair of forks, knives, and paper napkins. I bring out the ketchup from the refrigerator. "Anything else?" I sit down.

"Water. Glass of water."

"Oh!" I jump up and fill two glasses with water from the tap.

"Thank you. So...when are you going back?"

"Tomorrow, if the highway gets cleared up by then. I have to call Monica though."

"My mother would've been so proud of you. She wanted me to go to college, but...." She looks off into the window. "Snow's stopped."

The world outside is silent and white. The kitchen fills with the flavorful humidity of pasty. I inhale. Sometimes I swear that I'm a pasty junkie. "Smells really good."

"Of course. It's pasty time!" She chuckles but she suddenly stops.

"You okay?"

"Please promise me you'll finish college. Your mother tried, but she had you, and she couldn't.... Just don't have babies when you're not ready, you hear?"

"Of course not!" I am surprised by her indirect reference to the recent Roe v. Wade decision, which has been all over the news lately.

"Just you finish college. Don't marry until after you have a degree and a full-time, good-paying job. I don't want you to end up like me or your mother."

"No, I won't."

"Good." She glances at the kitchen clock. "What the hell. Let's go pasty now."

I use a burger flipper to bring pasty to plate and set the plates in front of us.

"Do you want a Yooper sticker?"

"Whyever for?"

"I got a bunch. Maybe you know people who'd want it for their cars."

"No."

"It's a big thing now. It's *our* word. We're Yoopers."

"Really?"

"Yes! Some people say we have our own culture."

"What culture?"

"Well, you know we have our own rules, the way we behave with each other—that sort of thing."

She squints at me. "Don't tell me that taking the day off from work on the first day of hunting season is...whaddya call it, Yooper culture?"

I burst out laughing.

"See? Some people need to get their noses out of 'em books and shovel some snow," she says. "We got plenty here. Three feet's a good start. Yooper culture."

"Oh, Grandma!" I have to wipe my eyes from having laughed so hard. "Some people are researching how we talk differently from everyone else. It's like a dialect. It's almost a whole new language!"

"Some guys out here talk funny," she says. "*Eh.*" She gives a dismissive wave. "Who cares about that?" She saws open her steaming pasty and points to the jar of ketchup. "Time to eat."

How Copper Came to the Keweenaw Peninsula

by Raymond Luczak

A long time ago Venus paid the Keweenaw Peninsula
a visit. She stepped off her gold-encrusted chariot
on the shore off Eagle Harbor. Her horses,
shimmering with the flaxen of sun, nibbled
at the wild plants that lined Lake Superior.

Indeed on this beautiful summer day, made for galloping
above the lilting waves, she rested.
She much needed a vacation alone from the chaos
after the Romans forced her half-sister Aphrodite
into exile. She was tired of being watched.

She gathered a bevy of raspberries and strawberries.
Her skin glowed with the flush of fresh blood.
Her toes nestled among agates that nuzzled.
She sat facing the western sun from a fallen log,
worn smooth as sandal against marble.

Up north the darkening skies spewed hues of color.
Her cousin Sagittarius galloped and shot arrows at stars,
not knowing that she was watching, or even missing.
Her horses settled down to sleep on the sand
next to her. The night air was her blanket.

After so many nights alone in bed, she'd thought
her husband Vulcan would never notice
the emptiness in their bed, or how she'd drifted
into loneliness as she saw how he banished
the rest of the Greek side of her family.

She suddenly heard a distant rumble of hooves
thundering from the east. She squinted at
the chariot silhouette of Vulcan whipping
his horses harder, faster, *now*. Her heart sank
when her horses didn't stop neighing fear.

As he stepped off his chariot, he didn't say
a word. His coal eyes shone the language of fire.
His shoulders were always smoking volcanoes.
He never drank water except to cool off and make love.
His thrusts blurred the line between passion and rage.

His skin, already limning yellow-orange,
was lined with the sweat beads of anger.
He vomited streams of lava bile at her.
But the first volley missed, landing near
Minnesota and Ontario, where it became Isle Royale.

His next expulsion melted down her chariot.
That second flowing just couldn't stop sizzling
everything south of Eagle Harbor except for her,
already floating on the clouds of steam,
weeping at what a stupid concubine she'd become.

He never let her out of his sight until she died.
Centuries later his lava bile became the richest copper,
the very metal that sparked alchemical explorations.
But one alloy after another never turned into gold.

He didn't care. He had drunk himself to death.

Raymond Luczak, a Yooper native with roots in Ironwood and Houghton, is the author and editor of nineteen books. His latest title is *The Kinda Fella I Am: Stories*, released in March 2018. His work has been nominated nine times for the Pushcart Prize. He lives in Minneapolis, Minnesota, and online at raymondluczak.com.

U.P. Reader is Accepting Submissions for Issue #3

◆❖◆

The Upper Peninsula Publishers and Authors Association (UPPAA) presents a new publication called the *U.P. Reader*. This will be an annual anthology that will feature the collected works of the best of the authors of the Upper Peninsula.

"The *U.P. Reader* is something I hope will put Upper Peninsula authors in touch with the readers to expand their exposure to a much greater and more effective level," commented Committee Chair, Mikel B. Classen.

This collection will be published by the UPPAA and will showcase the multitude of talent within the membership of the organization. The *U.P. Reader* will average 60,000 words and will include all genres of writing including short stories, non-fiction and poetry. Artwork and photography pertaining to submissions are encouraged.

The *U.P. Reader* will be available to booksellers as well as authors for sale and promotion. This will allow the members an opportunity to participate in a project that will not only showcase their talents as writers but also to get the finished product in front of readers so they can discover the U.P. authors that interest them no matter what their reading preference.

Submissions will be juried by a panel and those chosen will appear in the *U.P. Reader*. Authors chosen to be published in the anthology will see their submission published along with an author's bio to steer readers to more work by that author.

"This is a publication about discovery. Finding new favorites and maybe rediscovering some old ones too. I think it is underestimated how many really talented writers we have living right here in the U.P. and the Reader will be the place to find them." Said Mikel Classen.

Tyler Tichelaar, President of UPPAA, adds, "A collection of short stories, poetry, and essays will allow readers to enjoy a hodgepodge of U.P. literature from many different voices and will offer numerous visions and definitions of what it means to live here. The U.P. can be many different things to many different people and such a collection will help make that clear."

Proceeds from the *U.P. Reader* will be used to support operating costs of the UPPAA and its many events to educate its members about writing and publishing and to get U.P. literature into the hands of potential readers.

The deadline for submitting for the next issue of U.P. Reader will be November 15th, 2018.

"I'm really excited about what we've received so far," said Mikel Classen, project head for the *U.P. Reader*. "I really want to see more."

The *U.P. Reader* only accepts new material that has never appeared before in print, eBook, or on the web. Writers who submit previously published work will be dropped from consideration. For more information, including submission guidelines, contact: editor@UPReader.org or visit us online at http://upreader.org/

Rants of a Luddite

by Terri Martin

Simple Gifts
'Tis the gift to be simple, 'tis the gift to be free,
'tis the gift to come 'round where we ought to be;
And when we find ourselves in the place just right,
'twill be in the valley of love and delight.
When true simplicity is gained,
to bow and to bend we shan't be ashamed.
To turn, turn will be our delight
'til by turning, turning we come 'round right.

Known as the Shaker dancing song.
Composed by Shaker Elder Joseph Brack.

As a child, I walked the water's edge, eyes cast intently downward, searching for simple offerings from the lake, such as a good skipping stone or a smooth pebble of intense luster. My uncanny ability to spot such riches amongst the mundane was not particularly appreciated. "Look at this one!" I would shout enthusiastically, presenting the umpteenth Special Rock to my sister. "Uh huh," she would mutter, turning over on her beach blanket to even out her tan. I had to settle for displaying my collection on a piece of driftwood or a picnic table like a curious shrine. The stones rarely made it home because not only did my mother object to their gritty presence—especially in the washer where they invariably ended up—but once they dried they lost their sheen, thus their appeal.

After all, a rock was just a rock and could hold a kid's attention only so long before other, more dynamic attractions took center stage. You can stare at a rock and although it is argued that therein may exist some kind of non-organic life form, it will never move of its own volition or provide any real entertainment. In most any census, technology will always prevail over something so ordinary as a rock. It, along with other simple intrigues, could never compete with that 1950s attraction in the living room corner: the television. While our parents were wary of its presence, it eventually became an integral part of our lives, enhanced with the invention of TV dinners that could be heated in their disposable aluminum foil dish and consumed off TV trays that folded and stacked in the corner. Our biggest technological challenge was manipulating the broken dial with a pair of pliers to change to one of the three available channels. We enhanced poor reception with aluminum foil on the rabbit ears. Best of all, watching was free. Now we have a veritable movie screen, sitting in a special "entertainment" room—a technological sanctuary, if you will—with a split screen and a half-dozen remotes scattered throughout the area whose functions remain a mystery. There are literally hundreds of channels but we complain that *nothing* worthwhile is on. Also, there's that hefty monthly bill.

The Shaker dancing song, "Simple Gifts," reveres a simple lifestyle, and suggests that those who follow this path will live "in the valley of love and delight," which I interpret as a life and/or afterlife of peace and serenity. An offshoot of Quakers, the Shakers originated in 1747. When the spirit moved them, the Shakers could be quite physically demonstrative, allowing their faith to manifest itself in twitching, shaking, and dancing—thus the name Shaker. The Shaker society has suffered low enrollment, not entirely because of the simple gifts that they embrace, but more likely because of their belief in a celibate lifestyle. Early on they were able to adopt children into the society, but that eventually became illegal. Recruitment depended on word-of-mouth, and a life of all work and no fun was a hard sell. As of January, 2017, only two members of the Shaker society remained to dwell in the valley of love and delight at Sabbathday Lake, Maine. However, they do leave a legacy of wonderful songs and utilitarian furniture.

If you were to take a peek beneath the veneer of simplicity in a Shaker commune you would find a surprisingly complex culture, governed by an abundance of rules, traditions, and regulations that take the faithful a lifetime to learn. The Shaker society may initially appear to have been founded in the simple doctrine of equality and serving God. Folks lived in family units, they shared the fruits of their labor, and women and men were considered of equal importance in the eyes of God. Indeed, this sounds almost progressive except that each "family" was exclusively male or female, with the sexes segregated into separate living quarters. And although a proclaimed gender-equal society, the Shakers adhered to traditional gender roles, with women assigned to the domestic tasks of cooking, sewing, cleaning, and such while the men toiled in shops and fields. The abstention of sex was an ef-

fort to disassociate themselves from *women's* original sin. Hmm, maybe not so simple and delightful. Modern women would likely have their hackles up over this biblical elucidation.

This seemingly fundamental society is not alone in this inadvertent paradox. Complexity often lurks under the guise of good clean living. For example, camping is a form of outdoor recreation that eschews electricity and running water and returns us to nature, i.e. simplicity. We pitch a tent by the lake to remove ourselves from the stress of our everyday lives and soon all our cares become nothing but a faint echo. I recall my Girl Scout camp days of outdoor cooking, table lashing, campfire songs, and learning invaluable skills such as braiding plastic lanyards and treading water. Perhaps I confused the simplicity of my childhood with the act of camping. When the back-to-nature urge resurrected itself during my mid-life crisis, I took to the woods, searching for the simple gifts of God's creations. But the ground had gotten harder, the tent claustrophobic, and the weather— what with all this global warming mixed up with the next ice age—unpredictable. The solution: a thirty-foot recreation vehicle. As soon as we pulled out of the RV sales lot, we had inadvertently transformed the simplicity of camping into tedious disenchantment. Now our retreat into the wild— correction: entrance into the overcrowded modern campground (full hookup!)—had turned us 'round to the place where we had started: the world of worry, including an RV loan, insurance, camping fees, tangled extension cords, dump station lines, temperamental RV gadgets, and worst of all, backing into our designated campsite. Planning a camping trip was no longer throwing a few things into the back of the truck, but an *event*. Somewhere along the road, simplicity got complicated.

We cannot seem to help ourselves; it as if we are genetically programmed to do this.

RV camping notwithstanding, baby boomers, who came of age during simpler times, are wary, just as our parents were with the invention of the television, that we are witnessing a departure from social core values. We are annoyed and startled with the evolution of technology that has produced the new-fangled inventions that sit on every tabletop and jut from every pocket and purse, urgently binging, ringing, and dinging.

Millennials serve as a major target of the tech-mania, enticed by marketing schemes promising unlimited data and phones for everyone in the family. Mom can talk on the phone, bring up a dinner recipe on her computer, and watch Oprah at the same time. Dad simultaneously pays bills, watches the game, and shoots off a few emails to coworkers. The kids pretend to do homework on their laptops while texting friends and listening to music (earbuds in). Mom could set the kitchen on fire, smoke alarms screaming, and it's unlikely anyone would notice.

Human eye contact has become passé, replaced with a small, slick little computer that is never more than twelve inches from its owner. People strut along purposefully, eyes cast downward, texting. Others walk with phones pressed to their ears, blabbing about inconsequential things for all those around to overhear. Distracted drivers take side trips onto sidewalks and are only vaguely aware of the shouting as people leap to safety. Our world has grown smaller and smaller and we live within the confines of a 3x6-inch gadget that knows all, sees all, tells all. Library books gather dust, bookstores close, Christmas greetings and birth announcements come through social media, along with pictures of food, naughty pets, amusing children, and unsubstantiated news tidbits that send the gullible into indignant rants. Businesses communicate through automated phone systems that rarely offer human contact while customers listen to a detached recording telling them how important they are. Driverless cars will soon roll down an assembly line, allowing distracted drivers to text and talk to their heart's content, while the marvel of technology takes command of the wheel.

As we diverge further and further from the simplistic tools of our ancestors—hunting mammoths with pointy sticks and starting fires by smacking two rocks together—technology has quietly and steadily enslaved us. It's the new demigod: a metaphorical shiny pebble that has crept into every corner of our lives until there is no room left for our existence. We have come to believe that we *must* have these complex devices that will make life simple, easy, and meaningful.

The irony of life is that there is nothing simple about *anything*. What appears to be an unadorned plate of scrambled eggs is really a fussy omelet. When I start my day with the flip of a switch and a twist of the faucet, I do not yearn for the implied simplicity of a kerosene lantern and cold-water basin in which to perform my morning toilette. Not once in the middle of the night have I longed for a cold, dark trip to the outhouse in lieu of indoor plumbing, nor would I consider it "simple" to hitch the horse to a buggy as opposed to turning a key in the ignition of my Subaru, which is a technological marvel in itself. The simple life is an illusion, eluding definition, like an honest day's work or a good old-fashioned girl. Yet deep within my soul, I know that technology has become *too* important—a substitute for something basic and essential.

Just as the Shakers are all but extinct, so are the simple gifts, which are as fleeting as a skipping stone lost beneath the waves. The attempt to socially backpedal, to connect with God's plan, by eschewing those silicon demons that spread like a fungus, only leads us down a road of undeniable paradox because we are entrenched in technology and cannot take away that which we now have. Those who have tried going "off the grid" are labeled as nutcases, and since they know they can always go back if things don't work out, they could also be labeled as frauds. Perhaps true simplicity is found within the soul rather than worn on the sleeve. Due to a lack of insightful planning, we've not *come 'round right* but rather have stumbled into a world gone nutty with inventions that woo us like that shiny river rock, which all too quickly turns dull and uninteresting. No matter, there is another gleaming prospect just upriver, just past the valley of love and delight.

The Yooper Loop

by Terri Martin

Photo Credit - Nathan Miller, www.NathanInvincible.com

Michigan's Upper Peninsula offers all the quintessential north woods stuff: sparkling lakes and streams, a zillion acres of forests, bug-infested swamps, monumental snowfall, and other outdoorsy attractions offering endless opportunities for recreational wandering. All well and good, but we are overlooking a potentially revenue-generating attraction. Not only would it draw the average adventure-seeking tourist into our remote neck of the woods, but also very possibly attract a convention of traffic engineers to "experience" what is in my humble opinion a truly unique and totally unprecedented traffic conundrum known as "The Yooper Loop."

First, let me back up a bit and explain to non-locals that a "Yooper" is a resident of Upper Michigan (aka Upper Peninsula). See, you take the "U" and the "P" add an "er" to the end and you got your Yooper. We recently made it into the Merriam-Webster Dictionary, which simply describes "Yooper" as a slang word for residents of Michigan's Upper Peninsula. Much discussion has occurred among said U.P. residents who find the Merriam-Webster definition lacking. Various criteria are tossed about in an attempt to define the particulars of who can lay claim to this apparent badge of honor associated with being a Yooper. Some steadfastly claim one not only must be born and raised in the U.P. but (s)he must also have at least three consecutive documentable generations of family who were born and raised here as well. Extra points are given to those whose great-great ancestors came over on a boat to work in the mines. Some hold the opinion that these harsh guidelines discriminate, and the rule of thumb is that one must live here for twelve consecutive years, including winter, to proclaim Yooperhood. More progressive and philosophical thinkers believe that Yooper nirvana cannot be achieved by simply sticking it out for twelve years. To them, Yooper "enlightenment" is more about values and lifestyle, and perhaps capitulation to ridiculous winters and scant evidence of modern civilization. It's about *sisu* and suffering and hardship and hardiness and—did I mention suffering? It's about how to eat a pasty (with ketchup) and gut a deer and the proper inflection when ending a sentence with the expression: *eh?*

But I digress. We are talking about the Yooper Loop and its potential as a major revenue-generating tourist "trap." Come one, come all, see it twist, turn, and contort traffic into a writhing mass of chaos. Fun for the whole family! Once you've done it, you'll never be the same!

The Yooper Loop is a monstrosity of tangled highway involving US 41—a rather major and heavily used throughway—and M-26 coming to roost at the Portage Canal Lift Bridge. The bridge, an aging engineering marvel, is located in the Keweenaw Peninsula and connects Houghton to Hancock. It is the *only* bridge across the Portage Canal.

Even the most befuddling traffic circle is mere child's play compared to the Yooper Loop. While negotiating the Loop, drivers face many confusing options and illogical lane choices, as they play an exciting game of chicken with other equally confused drivers coming from other directions with similar challenges. It must be remembered that nearly everyone has the right of way, except the hapless backed-up lines of vehicles converging south of the bridge.

South-bounders who clear the bridge face some dicey lane changing. Here is the place where everyone has the right of way, and only the devilishly daring will prevail. Driv-

ers have been known to jut their heads out the windows shouting dibs or making other verbal comments that cannot be properly expressed with a simple toot of the horn or hand gesture. Using a turn signal only adds to the confusion.

Meanwhile, higher up on the M-26 intersection, those who simply wish to go south on 41 theoretically don't need to address the Loop. However, they will be competing with others zipping southbound over the bridge that are trying to access the outside, inside, or ambiguous center lane. They do this around a 90-degree traffic loop (thus its namesake) at a breakneck speed with lane choice often being random and fickle, causing a lack of communication with the south US 41 intenders. The experience is similar to a driver who has his right turn signal on and turns left. Confusion and, ultimately, traffic discordance is inevitable.

All others wishing to go north or south on US 41 are expected to just work things out when their lanes merge with no apparent favoritism to either party. Those heading southbound over the bridge typically are trying to, upon successfully crossing the bridge, get in the LEFT lane in order to continue their southward journey on US 41. Meanwhile, those coming out of Houghton on US 41 North who do not wish to cross the bridge, but instead want to take M-26 to Wal-Mart and other attractions, must get in the RIGHT lane. As these two warring factions converge, only the bold emerge victorious. Sparring for dominance often results in a total lack of congeniality and even disreputable gestures and other unsavory acts of road rage, not to mention the occasional traffic accident. Add a vigorous winter snowstorm, and you have something beyond mayhem.

Police have been known to request a mental health leave of absence after trying to conduct an accident scene investigation at the Yooper Loop. Our men and women in blue (or brown in the case of county constabulary) are under great pressure to make sense of the free-for-all of the Yooper Loop. At the very least, they are facing a tedious day in court trying to explain something that defies logic.

In order to keep the bridge in good working order, it undergoes major renovations and minor corrections (such as releasing crossing gates that refuse to go up). The seemingly ongoing construction also includes the approach ramps, which need to be torn up and replaced regularly. Naturally, this results in lane closures to allow the crews room to park every imaginable piece of road construction equipment while creating enormous piles of dirt and broken-up concrete. For some reason known only to them, they choose to begin the closure each day at the exact time that commuter traffic nears its peak. Naturally, this further contributes to the bottleneck created at the "Loop," and just for fun, workmen switch lanes back and forth lest drivers think they can plan ahead. Locals can get cocky, too, thinking they know the "ins and outs" of the Yooper Loop during construction. Each morning on their commutes, they switch to high alert as the inevitable road work signs come into view. These in themselves are deceptive, often proclaiming a lane closure or potential traffic backup, which doesn't exist. Because of this ambiguity, locals may tragically ignore warning signs only to find that they should have taken things more seriously and now they may be fined or imprisoned for civil or criminal disobedience, especially if it is not open season on construction workers.

The final caveat lies with the lift bridge itself, which has a purpose beyond simply getting folks to the other side. It is also designed to snarl traffic and push human endurance to the brink of insanity. A driver tools along 41, thinking about his or her business on the other side of the bridge when, WHAMMY: lights flash, bells clang, and the bridge crossing gate slowly and mockingly drops down. The typical closure lasts just a few minutes, but manages to cause an impressive traffic backup that essentially brings the Yooper Loop and roads stretching in all directions to a grinding halt. Nothing moves, including police, firetrucks, or ambulances heading to area hospitals. Those who are close to the gate get to watch. At first nothing appears to be happening. Then, almost imperceptibly, a portion of the bridge separates from the main structure and begins its ascent. While idling away, bemused motorists await something noteworthy to sail through, such as an aircraft carrier or platoon of Navy destroyers headed for North Korea, but instead a tiny sailboat appears on the horizon and can be seen inching its way up the canal. When the bridge finally reaches its apex, the boat slowly putts through, its mast appearing through the opening that the detached section has provided. The boat carries two people, probably from Chicago, and a Yorkshire Terrier that, while it can't be heard, is undoubtedly yapping its fool head off. Imagine raising tons of steel and halting countless vehicles, making attorneys late for court, doctors late for surgery, people late for work, school, lunch, hair appointments, dental visits, and their own weddings just to allow passage to a tiny pleasure sailboat! Once the passage is accomplished, there is another anxious waiting period when, again, nothing happens. It's as if the bridge has come *alive*, its rusty grid casting a wicked smirk to all who wish to pass over. Then slowly, hesitantly it begins its tedious, screeching descent back into place. Several US presidents come and go. Global warming reverses and an ice age converges. New species of flora and fauna appear and then go extinct. At last, the bridge shudders into place (except when it malfunctions). The gate lifts, allowing cars, bicyclists, pedestrians, and migrating herds of animals to resume their journeys.

With proper marketing, the Yooper Loop could become of the U.P.'s greatest tourist attractions and, perhaps, even be touted as one of the *Seven Wonder Whys of the World!* While some may conquer the labyrinth of twists and turns of the Loop, those who experience Portage Canal Lift Bridge Gridlock (PCLBG) can languish away in a place where time *literally* stands still. When they finally emerge, somewhat wild-eyed and speaking in tongues, that which seemed important upon entering the time warp, such as work, family, taxes, gasoline, etc., is exchanged for a new, more urgent priority: a restroom.

Yooper Loop · Winter view

Hah! Good luck with that. The next rest area is ninety miles up the road.

🧠 🧠 🧠

Terri Martin and her husband moved to the U.P. nearly eighteen years ago, and have no desire to live anywhere else. Terri is currently a regular contributor to *U.P. Magazine* (Porcupine Press) where she finds an outlet for her humorous writing. Terri has a published middle-grade children's novel, *A Family Trait.* Until her recent retirement, Terri worked in higher education and as a grant writer for a non-profit. She graduated from Western Michigan University in the 1970s and earned a master's degree in English from Northern Michigan University in 2013. She can be reached at terri4045@gmail.com.

About the Photo:

Nathan Miller wrote: "It's actually a funny story how I took the Yooper Loop photo. Rather than use a drone to carry a camera into the air, I hoisted them up with the help of big kites—kites as tall as a man! The cameras are attached to the string and soar into the air thanks to nothing but the wind. All I have to do is roam around and keep the kite out of trees or power lines. It's quite fun and a lot quieter than drones, though it does take a bit longer. In the case of the winter shots, I did those from out on the ice." You can see more aerial U.P. photography at www.NathanInvincible.com.

Roslyn Elena McGrath

Winded

She was woken by the wind,
its plaintive gusts resounding through the
    eaves
and battering the windows.

She was lifted up by the wind,
held suspended over twisted bed sheets
in her horizontal, at-rest position.

She was penetrated by the wind,
its wildness entering and loosening
the spaces between each cell.

She was sucked out into night sky by the
    wind,
through an unforeseen opening
in her bedroom wall.

She was carried off by the wind,
its currents dispersing pieces of her in ev-
    ery direction,
spreading her thinly, hugely, and nearly
    undetectably
throughout the planet, the stars, the gal-
    axy,
and places as yet un-thought of.

She was motivated by the wind,
lifting as it lifted, soaring as it soared,
crashing as it crashed.

She was educated by the wind,
touching what it touched,
finding what it found.

She was swept back toward herself by the
    wind,
as it gathered her particles
into a shimmering pile of vibrations.

She was re-shaped by the wind,
each piece of her transfigured
by its expanded experiences.

She was reunited by the wind,
each aspect of her newfound being
swirled into stronger connection with all
    the others.

She was revealed to herself by the wind,
as it tumbled over new contours
and hushed against soft edges.

She understood herself through the wind,
mimicking its patterns, bending with its
    currents,
and listening to its ancient, changing voice.

She was brought back to herself by the
    wind,
rolling inward with its wake and touching
    the spaces within spaces within spaces
    inside herself.

She was made whole by the wind,
as it stirred inward with outward,
spinning all together in a blend beyond
    imagining.

She was poured out by the wind,
adding more glimmer to star shine and
    dewdrops,

more lilt to its song.

Roslyn Elena McGrath

Stop Clocks

Stop all the clocks!
Allow them tyranny over my life, my
    breath,
the core of my being no more,
so that I may stretch into the knowing
of my oneness with the Universe,
feel my edges brush against
the farthest corners of creation,
and my heartbeat sing in endless
    harmonies!

Stop all the clocks that have caused me
to count days, minutes, and hours,
forward and back, keeping track
of everything except the now.

Clocks stop and whisper
about the past and the future,
pointing their fingers at areas
of shame, blame, worry and
    forgetfulness,
arguing about whose millisecond
is most accurate, and talking about one
    another
in Standard, Eastern & Daylight Savings
    time.

Stop clocks,
listen
to the one-verse
within the heart of all be-ings,
Is-ings, now-ings
and corroborate our knowing
that time is just an allusion to reality.

Stop clocks wait
in measured time
knowing that what is asked for
can never be given—
eternity is meaningless
without a knowing of its falsification
and condensing down into seconds,
minutes,
hours.
A moment is all you need to be.

Marquette, MI resident **Roslyn Elena McGrath** is the author of five personal growth and healing books and the publisher of *Health & Happiness U.P. Magazine.* Her poems, short stories, and essays are inspired by her sense of the magic embedded in the world, her experiences with nature, spirituality, and inner healing, and the creative nourishment of her writing group. You can find out more about her books and healing work at www.Empowering Lightworks.com.

Slip of the Lip

by Becky Ross Michael

"You awake?" Soft breath tickled the woman's ear.

"Wha?" Words failed to form in her mouth devoid of saliva. She spotted a glass of water on the nightstand and swallowed a gulp. Beyond the edges of the thick comforter, the room was frosty. She glanced over the bedside and saw a young, dark-haired girl gazing back at her. A somewhat older, fair-haired version joined them in the room wearing an expression of both joy and worry.

"We made you some toast," the blonde girl said, raising a paper napkin holding more butter than bread.

"I don't..." started the woman.

"The baby's tryin' to climb over the side of her bed," the older girl continued. "Dad said he was goin' to play basketball. I changed her diaper in the crib, but didn't know if I should take her out."

"I better check," suggested the woman, rising from the bed and noting that she had slept in corduroy jeans, a long-sleeved T-shirt, and thick white socks.

The woman brushed the walls with her fingertips to calm the swaying that assailed her, as they walked down a short hallway together. Upon entering a smaller bedroom decorated with bright wallpaper, the youngest child stood and began shaking the rail, light brown hair standing on end, as if electrified. "Mama-mama-mama," she repeated with a wide, toothless grin.

The woman searched the oldest girl's green eyes.

"Remember us?" the girl whispered.

"Don't be silly," the woman replied, lifting the youngest sister from a dark wooden crib.

"It seemed like you were gone for a long time," said the middle girl, trailing the small group from the room.

"Just a little while can feel like forever," the woman evaded.

Upon entering the kitchen, a snowy scene greeted her outside the large window. On a calendar hung low from the wall, dates leading to a Friday in December were each crossed out in a childish scrawl. A flyer for an arts-and-crafts show hung next to it on a corkboard. She placed the baby in a highchair, turned up a nearby thermostat, and walked over to inspect the refrigerator's contents.

Breakfast was a confusion of canned fruit, toast, and cold cereal drenched in the remnants of a milk carton. They ate out of mismatched containers, since most bowls and plates from the cupboards crustily decorated the countertops and one side of the sink. The middle child chattered and regaled the woman with snippets about a series of babysitters, while the toddler banged with a spoon on the tray of her highchair. The oldest girl didn't say a word and studied the familiar stranger at their table.

The awkward morning passed, even though complicated by details that remained beyond the woman's reach. "Baba, baba," the little one begged and placated herself by sucking on a bottle of watered-down apple juice retrieved from under a chair. After giving up

2018 | Issue #2

her quest of navigating the living room, she plunked down on her diapered bottom with a wide yawn and soon fell asleep on the worn carpet. The oldest grabbed an afghan from a nest on the sofa, where someone must have slept the previous night, and with a motherly pat covered the dozing youngster. The woman agreed when the middle child asked if she could go down in the basement to ride her bike.

"I'm Tina, and that's Linda, downstairs. The little kid's Nora." Seeing the slight nod of acknowledgment from the woman, the girl offered, "You told me, once, that you ended all our names with an 'a' because your mom's name was like that."

Seeing another flicker of recognition, Tina said, "Sometimes you liked lookin' at our baby books and stuff from over there," and pointed with a chewed thumbnail at a shelf. "I didn't like it that daddy made you cry," she added, before she headed down the stairs to join her sister.

Tears closed the mother's throat and stole any possible reply.

The afternoon was a treasure hunt. She moved in slow motion, while sifting through folders in an organizer on the kitchen counter and drawers of a small desk, finding past-due utility bills and Tina's school papers printed with care. When she came upon hospital invoices and insurance correspondence, she noted the designation, "Patient name: Elizabeth."

The woman opened a purse that was set on top of a free-standing kitchen cabinet, saw several dollars in the change compartment, and took a long look at a driver's license resting alongside the money.

After removing several prescription bottles from another zippered section, she examined the labels and scanned her recent memories. She hesitated for a few seconds, dumped their contents into the kitchen sink, and watched the rainbow of capsules swirl and begin to dissolve in a torrent of hot water. The medicinal odor reached her nostrils, and memories of a stark and lonely room began to surface. Bile rose in the woman's throat, and she vomited into the basin watching the last of the pills circle the drain.

She then sat cross-legged on the floor and leafed through baby books filled with hope and family picture albums telling the story of another lifetime. Her brimming eyes stared into the smiling faces.

Returning to the room where her journey had begun that morning, the unmade bed offered temptation of surrender. She ached to lie down, close her eyes, and stop trying to remember. Instead, her eyes focused on the surface of a dresser. She lifted a rectangular wooden box that smelled of cedar and hunted for a tool to open the lock. After resorting to a paperclip, she opened the box and peered through small plastic envelopes at tiny, pearl-like baby teeth and glanced at greeting cards saved from long-forgotten occasions. At the bottom, a slip of paper lay folded. "If you go to the game tonight, is Beth coming, too?" It was signed, "Natalie." *Natalie?* More questions than answers.

Car tires sounded outside the house on a snow-packed driveway. She snapped the lock into place and returned to lengthening shadows in the living room. The tempo of her heart accelerated.

Upon entering the room, the man's eyes slid away from hers. "Sorry about the dishes and laundry, Beth. I meant to do all that before you got home last night...."

"I need to get something from the store," she interrupted. "It won't take me long. Tina and Linda are playing with Nora in her room."

"I'm not even sure you're supposed to drive, yet, Beth, and it's getting a little slippery out. I'll do it instead," he insisted.

"It's okay. I'll just go to the nearest place."

"Let me at least make sure the driveway's clear enough for you to get out," he said and headed back outside.

With a flash of irritation, she scooped keys from the desk, retrieved her purse, and grabbed a hooded jacket and gloves from hooks on the wall. The moment he returned, she hurried out the door.

Beth held her breath, and the light car balked in the deepening snow when she tried to back out of the driveway toward the street. She wasn't surprised that he hadn't cleared the way, after all, and a shadow that appeared in a window of the house next door caught her attention for a moment. Rocking the vehicle between reverse and drive, she finally was free.

As Beth drove, her headlights cut through the escalating snowstorm, and she recognized passing streets and buildings as if awakening from a hazy dream. At a sharp curve in the road, she visualized the dark river beckoning from beyond a tall stand of pines. Driving past the first little shop with a flickering entrance light, she slid to a stop at the second.

Beth wore no boots and picked her way through slush in the small parking lot before entering the market. She soon returned and moved to place the container of milk on the front seat. Without knowing why, she stepped back into the swirling flakes and opened the trunk of the car.

There she discovered two handcrafted ceramic pots under an old woolen blanket. Beth removed her gloves to caress the pottery's rough lines and noticed the vessels were room temperature. Considering her options, she decided to leave them in place and slammed the trunk closed. Mentally arranging the pieces to fit, Beth followed tire tracks through the snow, in return to someone's life, if not her own.

"June's on the phone," Tina announced, pressing the device Beth had left behind into her hands when she entered the warmed kitchen. The woman placed the milk in the refrigerator with a pounding heart and took a deep breath.

Words from the other end could have cut, but instead sounded reassuring through the stress roaring in her ears. "Several people saw him with Natalie buying pottery at the arts-and-crafts show, of all places, today. You're much stronger than you know, Beth."

Her friend's voice was familiar and treasured, like a song recalled from childhood. She envisioned many hours spent next door with June, sharing endless cups of coffee and personal revelations, with the children dancing around them.

"Thanks so much," she replied into the phone. After ending the call, Beth glanced over at her three daughters, who played amid a sea of building blocks in the soft, yellow circle of lamplight. Tina's solemn eyes met her own. The man looked up from the television and blushed over what he guessed was a new disclosure.

The volume from a blaring sports event faded into the background. Beth's field of vision narrowed, and she peered down a long, dark passageway. Accepting the truth, her view then brightened, as vague uncertainties rearranged into recognizable order.

She descended the basement stairs and picked her way between bicycles, roller skates, and piles of laundry on the cement floor. Beth found what she wanted high on a dusty shelf. He met her at the top step when she returned and followed her along the hallway to the room they had shared. She opened the large suitcase on top of the bed and then hesitated.

"At least you can take the kids with you this time," he said.

"I'm not the one who's leaving," she answered.

A memory spread before her with the same clarity as the moment it occurred. She had sat, folding laundry in a beam of sunlight that slanted through the blinds, while inhaling the warm sweetness of just-washed baby clothes. Her husband had come home from work in the middle of the day and claimed that they needed to talk.

"I love you, Natalie," he had mistakenly begun.

Becky Ross Michael writes tales and truths for both children and adults. Life has led her to various locales, but began in Michigan. Years later, she was fortunate to have lived and taught in the Upper Peninsula. Becky currently lives in North Texas, where she writes, leads a critique group, and works as an online editor. Her blog may be found at https://platformnumber4.wordpress.com/ and she welcomes visitors.

The Legend

by Shawn Pfister

t would have been an amazing legend, Macy realized as she listened to her grandmother's shame-filled story. It was totally epic; it had everything: mystery, betrayal, love.

"She was only thirteen," Grandma Agatha said sadly. "Just a child."

"What happened?" Macy asked, sitting cross-legged on the floor in front of her grandmother's La-Z-Boy. Her cell phone sat on the coffee table next to her, forgotten as she listened further to her grandmother's story.

"Thirteen. Only a year younger than you are now."

"Yeah, yeah, I get that," Macy added hurriedly, trying to speed the story along.

"They didn't know any better. It was a simpler time. They were simple folk," Agatha explained, more for her own benefit than for Macy's. Her hands were in her lap, idly playing with the hem of her sweatshirt. She looked up suddenly. "It doesn't matter, though. There is no excuse for doing that to a child."

"Doing what?" Macy was getting anxious. Grandma Agatha seemed to be stalling at this point in the story. She had gotten the back-story good, talking about the early days in the Soo and how their family went back to the founding homesteaders. It was all quaint and, in all honesty, a bit boring until Agatha mentioned Constance. That's when Agatha got all choked up and couldn't seem to bring herself to finish any more. Macy didn't even know who Constance was,

yet her grandmother was stalling so much. Constance was nothing more than a name to Macy.

Macy still wasn't sure what this story had to do with the large hope chest sitting in the living room next to her grandmother's La-Z-Boy. It was an old oak chest that Macy had never seen before, which astounded her. She thought she had been through every inch of her grandmother's house by now. How could she have missed something so large?

"They murdered her."

"What? Why? Who?" Macy asked, interest in the story quickly returning. "What could a thirteen-year-old girl in Sault Ste. Marie in 1713 have possibly done to get murdered?"

"She walked into town in the middle of the night, dazed and confused and covered in blood."

"Creepy," Macy admitted. "But that's more of a help-the-girl situation than a kill-the-girl situation."

"It was on the thirteenth day of the year in 1713. She was thirteen."

"Superstitious much?"

"On top of all those thirteens, she was clad in only her shift."

"Her what?"

"It's like a slip, maybe a little thicker," Agatha explained. "It was an undergarment."

"In January?" Macy was shocked.

Agatha nodded. "And the blood wasn't hers. Not one drop of it. A local woman, our ancestor," Agatha beamed with pride, "managed to talk them into letting her live. She took the girl home and cleaned her off and found absolutely no scratches on the child, not so much as a broken fingernail. However she came to be covered in blood did not involve her so much as having to defend herself."

"Freaky."

"The first whispers said 'witch,'" Agatha explained. Anticipating Macy's question, she added, "They were simple, religious people; they believed in such things."

Macy leaned forward, anticipating that something was to follow. Witch was too easy, too obvious, too made up.

"But when dawn broke, the girl panicked, expressing an extreme fear of the sun."

"Vampire?" Macy asked, excited. It was too good to be true. Her grandmother was telling her a vampire story. This was going to be awesome.

"They were simple people," Agatha defended them weakly. It seemed to be her defense for everything.

"Oh, my Go...goodness," Macy corrected herself quickly, seeing her grandmother's eyes close to slits.

"The townspeople were up in arms. They wanted to kill her during the day, when she'd be at her weakest. Our ancestor, hearing the calls of the mob, wrapped the girl in a heavy blanket to protect her from the sun and led Constance into the woods and away from their pitchforks and torches."

"Rock on, Uber-great Grandma."

Grandma Agatha lifted an eyebrow. "In her skirts, our ancestor had hidden a single wooden stake."

"No."

"She had small children to protect." Finally, a real defense. "The mob would have burned her house down with them in it in case they'd been turned into vampires, too."

"No."

"After they ran for several miles, they stopped under the shade of a large evergreen. She told the girl to rest, that she was safe, and, once she was sure the girl was asleep, she took out the stake and drove it deep into the girl's heart."

"But Grandma—"

Grandma Agatha did not stop and did not acknowledge that Macy had spoken. She just continued on, staring forward, too ashamed to look at Macy. "She walked home and told the mob that the girl had escaped her and headed south. They were angry at her, but glad the girl was gone and no longer their problem. So they all soon headed to their respective homes and, eventually, forgot about the event.

"Later, under the darkness of the moon and armed only with a single candle to guide her path, our ancestor made her way back to the spot under the evergreen.

"The still body of the young girl was exactly how she had left it, untouched by wildlife or decay."

"Creepy."

"Our ancestor believed this to be the body of a vampire, a dark and evil creature, not the fictionalized tragic heroes you see popularized today, and wanted to make sure the body would not return to life."

"What did she do?"

"She picked up the cold corpse and dragged it all the way to her home. It took her most of the night to do this on her own. Once she had the corpse in her house, she didn't know what to do with it. She wracked her brain and finally came up with a solution." She paused, lost in thought.

"Well?" Macy asked, needing to hear.

Grandma Agatha brushed her hand over the hope chest beside her absently. It was the first time all night she had so much as acknowledged its presence. Macy recoiled at the idea that popped into her head.

"She emptied out her hope chest and put the body in."

Macy's eyes fixated on the hope chest next to her grandmother. "That?" She pointed to it.

"Yes."

"Eww. That had a dead girl in it?" Macy scrunched up her face in disgust. "You can't seriously be giving that to me."

Agatha sighed. "It's your time to watch over it now," she explained. "I'm getting too old for it, and your mother doesn't have the stomach for something like this."

"But, Grandma, it had a dead girl in it."

"Correction," her grandmother stated sadly as she stood and pulled a key out of her pocket. "It has a dead girl in it."

Logging team with horses

"Gross," Macy said. She half smiled and added, "Not funny, Gram. You almost got me, tho...."

Her voice trailed off as the lid lifted and she gazed upon the face of a young girl.

"Next year will mark her three hundredth year in this box," Agatha said. "And, if not for the piece of wood in her chest, I'd swear she's sleeping merely." Agatha rubbed a soft finger lovingly over the girl's peaceful face.

"Grandma?" Macy took a step back in fear.

"Macy, I'd like you to meet Constance. We don't know her real name, obviously, but the women of our family have dubbed her Constance. She's your responsibility now. Good luck."

This would have made a great legend, Macy thought. A truly amazing town legend, but the secret was now hers and hers alone.

Raised in Michigan, **Shawn Pfister** now lives in Ontario. Shawn is a painter and photographer, but writing is her true passion. Shawn has published *My Vampire Prom Date and Other Stories*, a book of short stories, and is a featured writer in several anthologies including the LGBTQ charity anthology, *For Love of Leelah*, the werewolf anthology, *I Believe in Werewolves,* the vampire anthology, *Vicious Bites*, and the ghost anthology, *Vicious Spirits*. Shawn's stories speak, not only to the kid in your house, but to the kid in you! For more of Shawn's work, check out oppositeofpeople.org.

MEMBER BENEFITS:

Your Invitation to join the UPPAA Today

- Network with more than one hundred members of the publishing community
- Attend publishing/writing conferences and meetings
- Meet experts in the publishing industry!
- Receive the quarterly UPPAA newsletter, *The Written Word*
- Get discounts on IBPA and APSS Publisher Association Memberships
- Participate in the UPPAA email group for answers to all those publishing and marketing questions
- List your books & book covers at www.uppaa.org
- Display books at UPPAA tables at UPPAA meetings & other UP book events
- Learn the do's and don'ts of self-publishing
- Receive notice of upcoming book contests and awards
- Submit work for publication to the annual UP Reader magazine

Join now at http://uppaa.org/join-or-renew/

WHAT IS UPPAA?

UPPAA is the Upper Peninsula Publishers and Authors Association.

WHEN WAS UPPAA FOUNDED?

- The organization began in 1998 when Sue Robishaw, wishing to share her self-publishing experiences and learn from others, had the idea to form UPPAA. With the help of Lynn Emerick and Michael Marsden, the first UPPAA Conference was held in June 1998 at Northern Michigan University with thirty people in attendance.
- Since the organization's founding, UPPAA has grown to more than 100 members, representing a diverse body of writers in the fields of fiction, nonfiction, history, children's books, science and many other fields. You can view our members' books at www.uppaa.org.

WHAT IS UPPAA'S PURPOSE?

UPPAA was founded with the purpose to support and encourage networking and idea exchange among Upper Peninsula, and surrounding area, publishers and authors, and to promote books published and/or authored by UPPAA members.

DOES UPPAA HAVE MEETINGS?

- An annual conference is held in the spring and regular monthly meetings are also held. The meetings are held centrally in Marquette to provide convenience to members throughout the vast peninsula.
- The conference is usually divided into several workshops, focusing on such topics as writing, the mechanics of publishing, publishing cost-effectively, marketing, and publicity. UPPAA has also brought in internationally known guest speakers to its conferences, including Dan Poynter, Patrick Snow, Jerry Simmons, and Irene Watson.
- Attendance at conferences is free to UPPAA members.

HOW IS UPPAA ORGANIZED?

UPPAA is a non-profit organization with a Board of Directors. Board positions are open to any members and board members are nominated and voted in every two years by members.

WHAT IS UPPAA'S FUTURE?

With a group of enthusiastic and innovative members, UPPAA continues to grow and seek new ways in the rapidly changing world of book publishing to promote its Upper Michigan authors and their books.

At Camp: When the Cat Is Out of the House

by Christine Saari

◆❖◆

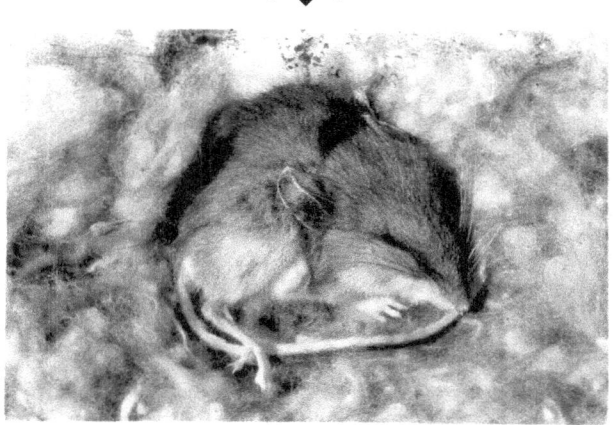

They gnawed their way into the silverware drawer
and bored a hole into our mattress.
They built a nest in the Coleman stove
and hid in Jon's Chinese slippers.
They tore the tassels off the rug on the wall
and chewed the candles to pieces.
They pulled threads out of the tablecloth fringe
and knocked the gourd off the shelf.
They built pathways into the blueboard
to chase each other at night.
They ripped grandmother's hand-sewn quilt
and hid seeds in the coffee grinder.
They left a nest of ten naked newborns
behind pots and pans in the dry sink.

Fed up, we resolved to fight the galling critters.

We tried to drive them out by sonic repeller,
but the high-pitched sound did not do the trick.
We set up traps underneath the bed,
behind the chest, in every corner.
The mice ate the morsels of cheese,
but the springs did not snap.
As a last resort we built a Finnish device,
wired a rolling log across a five-gallon bucket,
smeared peanut butter on it and made a ramp.
The mice crawled onto the log, fell in the bucket
and drowned. After we found twelve dead in the water
our pity got the best of us.

We gave up and left the mice alone.

Habitat

by Christine Saari

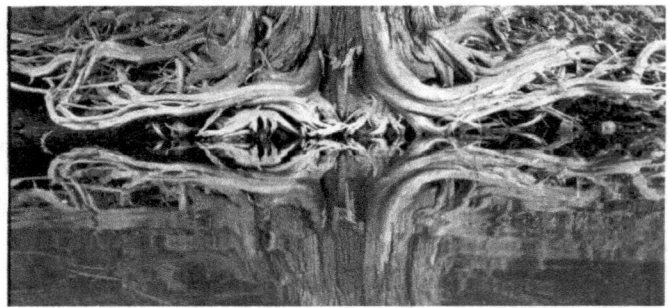

The ugly piece of fabric
draped over a fallen tree
in the Whitefish River,
has irked us for years.
Plants grow on it by now.

We decide to stop the canoe,
pull the waterlogged jacket
off its resting place.
We feel virtuous about restoring
the river's beauty.

As we near our landing we discover
three crayfish happily swimming in our boat.
When we drag the stinking garment unto land
a large frog emerges from its sleeve,
blinking and dazed.

In our excitement to clean up the Whitefish
we have disturbed the habitat
of invisible creatures.
Is this a lesson to look below the surface,
to leave things alone?

Christine Saari, a writer and visual artist, grew up in Austria and has lived in the Upper Peninsula since 1971. As a freelance journalist, she reported for Austrian newspapers as well as local magazines and newspapers across the U.P. Her 2011 memoir *Love and War at Stag Farm: The Story of Hirschengut, an Austrian Mountain Farm 1938-1948* covers the formative years of her childhood. Her debut poetry book *Blossoms in the Dark of Winter* was released in 2018. Her poems have appeared in *U.P. Reader Issue #1, Maiden Voyage, Water Musi, The Great Lakes State Poetry Anthology,* and *Me as a Child Poetry Series.*

Inception Through a Shared Fantasy

by T. Sanders

As a child, I had dreams of going fast. At first by running but later in life, I used some kind of mechanical assistance. Cars and boats were the most exhilarating. For a short time, I considered trains. That is until I learned respect and to fear them from my father.

He was a switchman on the Chicago & Northwestern Railroad and part of his job was to stop kids on their way to school from crossing to closely in front of switch engines. He had nightmares for years about narrow escapes kids had when they did not look or listen.

One lesson I remembered leaving a big impression on me happened on a summer day. My dad took me along to work with him on a Saturday. On the way to the end of the switchyard, we passed a mangled car off to the side of the tracks. Hit on the driver's side, it was now in the shape of a boomerang. When I asked what happened to the driver, my dad said, "Well...he lived."

We got to the yard office and sitting next to it was a steam engine. It was "stoked up" and was waiting to go to the west end of the yard to be dismantled and scrapped. My dad talked to the engineer for a few minutes and then called me over to ask if I wanted to ride with them to the other end of the switchyard. I could not refuse.

At first as the engine gained speed, it was an exciting ride but it got worse. With increased speed, it got noisier and smellier and shook my stomach into knots. When the stop block was in view at the end of the sid-

ing, the engineer finally bled the steam to the cylinders. He hollered at me to throw the brake. The only thing I could see in front of me was something that looked like a Model-A brake. Even though it looked backward, it worked. Immediately the engine began losing speed as it began jerking to a slow stop. Each stopping motion threw the total weight of my body against the brake arm. With each recoil, a sound like a dying deer or rabbit squeal was let out from the wheels catching up to the sand that had been sprayed on the rails. The duration decreased from the first one of thirty seconds to the last of about three.

After the engineer finished shutting down the engine, he took me to the front to see how the 80-ton iron dinosaur had finished its last assignment. The cowcatcher had come to rest eight inches from the stop block. He told me I should try not to come that close to the terminus ever again. In the next four thousand or so miles of train travel, I never did.

Thirty years later, I still had some of an appetite for speed. At this time I had a good enough job to indulge my taste for speed. I was a contractor of sorts with three assistants. A year's experience at a rural regional planning agency gave me the necessary skills to coordinate the state funding sources with mistrusting local government recipients.

The four of us worked out a system for the eighteen-hour days we had covering evening meetings, gathering and submitting data, and resubmitting funding applications. Three of us used the in between compensatory time to go back to school. I even had the luxury of fixing up the family vehicle, a Volkswagen bus with a modified Porsche engine. It was the perfect "sleeper car" to avoid tickets.

However, I may have gone too far stretching that envelope. On a car parts scavenging patrol, I found a deal for a modest sports car I had lusted for, ever since seeing it in a James Bond movie. I felt almost halfway to heaven.

A twinge of insecurity hit me almost immediately. Looking back at my life, maybe I was halfway to hell. I was thoroughly convinced when my wife got her second ticket driving the Spitfire. My insurance man showed up on my porch with a notice that my rate had doubled. As he walked away, I am sure I saw horns protruding out of his hair and the end of a pointed tail hanging out from his pants leg.

The last straw was when I started having a recurring nightmare. It was in a junkyard where a guard dog was barking. When it saw me, it gave chase. At first, it looked like a large yellow lab, but as it closed the distance between us, I could see it was orange not yellow, and the closer it got to me, black stripes became more apparent. My only hope of escaping the tiger was to make it to a slow-moving Ford station wagon a few yards ahead with its tailgate down.

Each time I had it, the dream ended in one of two ways. The first way, grabbed by the ankle, I woke up before hitting the ground. In the second, I would make it into the car, but when I crawled to the front, I found the tiger was driving with one paw and batting at a crucifix hanging from the rearview mirror with the other paw. In this version, I woke when the car crashed.

By mid-summer, fortunes had spun back around to the positive. At our meeting to close out the current year's project with a final review, we got an invitation for next year's project at the same time. Those of us who were in school had finished for the year and spirits and motivation could not have been higher.

On the day of the meeting, Sandra, the Admin-Asst., and I left for the state capital resolved to take the most scenic route. We took the Spitfire to take advantage of the perfect weather. I suggested she drive there and her obvious excitement increased by the mile.

The project review was nearly perfect save one item. Total cost billed for the project was about a hundred dollars less than allocated in the grant. That could cause an enormous paperwork headache. The auditor offered a solution that would make everyone happy. We stopped for lunch at a restaurant he recommended and had the most expensive things on the menu. At the Edgewater Hotel, we had sautéed thimbleberry crepes and truffles flambé with a sherry recommended by the maître d'. We got the restaurant receipt, a voucher for mileage, and left to get started on next year's work.

Carefully I began the drive home while Sandra napped. After fifteen minutes of silence, I decided to take a detour to let her share an experience, which was one of the reasons I bought the car we were driving.

A few miles from our office, there was a transfer terminal for semis. I visited it enough to find a trailer the same as one in the 007 movie I liked. With a tape measure I made sure it had the clearances needed.

She was still not fully awake when I turned at the entrance of the terminal. I then took a winding path around the target trailer to check the tires were fully inflated. The height markers on the parking wheel carriage were still undisturbed and the perpendicular alignment pop cans were still fastened and unmoved, nor were there any obstructions in the intended path.

Now fully awake, Sandra asked where we were. After explaining our exact location, I asked if she would like to re-enact a scene from a Bond movie. She agreed, probably feeling adventurous from the drinks at lunch.

I started to drive in a clockwise circle getting nearer the target trailer. When the circling motion was 270 degrees of a circle with the car facing the marked side of the trailer, I gave warning, "Don't stand up and

Logging the Hurricone River

keep your hands inside the car." We inched forward gradually accelerating as Sandra grabbed my leg and the dashboard chicken bar while calling out a series of syncopated, "Oh!s in tune and tempo increasing with the speed. Passing under the trailer, her moans turned into one long "Aaahhhh!" She gave a long sigh after we exited. Her last utterance after a hearty laugh was, "Now I remember that scene."

On the way back to the office, she asked if she might stop at home to check on something. Waiting in the car while Sandra was inside, I noticed the seat cover was wet. I got a large shop rag from the glove box and placed it on the seat. I noticed on the last leg of our trip she had changed her clothes and was wearing a smile that hinted at confidence, satisfaction, or both.

The first order of business back at the office was Sandra's announcement that she had received in the mail the final settlement check from her divorce. Second was for me to get out the travel voucher per the auditor's instructions. Sandra brought me everything ready to sign and mail. With it, was an envelope with my name containing a twenty-dollar bill with an explanation:

"My share for the surreptitious date today. The first of my new life.

—S

P. S. Put it toward a new seat cover."

🧠 🧠 🧠

Terry Sanders, is currently living in Manistique, MI, since retirement from work as a mechanical designer, environmental technician, and contractor preparing operation and assembly manuals. He received a BA from University of Wisconsin. Publications include: *High School Textbook for Mythology*, short works of fiction presented to workshops at the 2nd Saturday writers group in Curtis, MI, and a modern novella version of *The Iliad*.

Gregory Saxby

On the Circuit

On the circuit,
ground level;
Roads to everywhere
and nowhere.

Through places overflown
and overlooked,
the people
hidden from view;
the ones nobody knows
except for a few.

Places where spirits find
their harbors,
out of the wind,
out of the cold.

Places where their stories
can grow old
in wiser ways.

The places where
the wise ones know
that where two or three
may gather,
loving peace will grow.

The Last Tear

The last tear that drops
from swollen eyes,
at the end.

The last tear that drops
from swollen skies,
at the end.

The stubborn tears
that I cry for her,
at the end,
at the end.

The heart that
will not mend,
the oak that
will not bend.

I stand with them,
strong rooted in love.

I will not bend.

I stand with them,
to the last tear that drops
from my swollen eyes;
to the last light that shines
under swollen skies.

At the end,
At the end,
At the end

that never comes.

Gregory John Saxby resides in Goulais River, Ontario, twenty miles north of the twin Saults. He has performed his poetry at numerous open mics in the twin Sault, including Bayliss Library Poetry Cafe, Gore St. Cafe, and Superior Cafe. In January 2018, he published *Sipping Tea*, a collection of poems with a focus on the death of his wife, Diana, in 2015. On February 15, 2018, a reading and book signing for *Sipping Tea* was held at the Sault Ontario Centennial Library to benefit ARCH—the Algoma Regional Community Hospice.

Ar Schneller

Twinkle Twinkle Imaginary Star

how I wonder where you are
ancient supernova heading for earth
makes us wonder what our lives are worth
will your metallic iron heart be complete
with nothing left to claim defeat
will you flood the heavens with your light
when you dim it all one final night

distance has taken its toll
an extragalactic supernova
no swifter messenger
all roads lead into space
to explore its deep past
an eyewitness to evolution
a magic carpet ride on a bright comet's tail
traveling to the edge of the universe
past seventy billion trillion stars
our naked eye sees less than that
misunderstood by the future of man

there's a vibrant colorful world beyond
filled with a spectrum of energies
the heavens, x-rays and a big black hole
the unseen realm, the Big Bang afterglow
the solar system, our universe
push us past it all, take us to the cosmos
to touch crystal spheres and stillborn planets
speckled carpets of stars to infinity
unlock an endless night sky
full of unimaginable panoramic vistas

icy comets that orbit Jupiter and Neptune
will fall into the sun's orbit and explode
to limit our hazy vision then cloud our thoughts
war will plunge us into darkness, our final horizon
to struggle in a universe without stars or northern lights
ending all that we know to become a flash of radiation
to go no further, a civilization permanently etched
into walls of Iron and no more wood

Ar Schneller

Dying to Know

Death is easier to accept
and understand
when it's not your own
as we assist the elderly

advocate angels
families fly into town
to meet doctors, caregivers
and underpaid CNAs

with unspoken thoughts of dying
we pray for recovery
but most don't push past
handicap doors of nursing homes

aching bodies pulled
from comfort of reclined beds
that suck energy and life
wrinkled sheets create bedsores

watching loved ones cry
with brittle bones, sore backs,
weak arms, fragile soft minds
to upright positions in chairs

they sink slowly, not hungry
staring at their bed
wishing to crawl back in
as darkness enters the room

unable to abandon
wheelchairs, walkers,
gowns and commodes
unrealistic wishful thinking

wanting to return home
for the weekend
but unable to clean
or care for themselves

sleepy, groggy, too many drugs
they slip into not knowing
if it's day or night
eyes open or shut

nightmares tick with time
while fighting fearful thoughts
it's a one-way ticket up or down
to hell's eternity or pearly gates

Ar Schneller, a third generation Yooper, lives along the shores of Lake Superior near Little Girl's Point. U.P. scenery, life experiences, and people inspire her poetry, writing, photography, and art. Currently she writes and creates copper jewelry at her Downtown Art Place Studio in Ironwood. Learn more at www.Yooperlife.com

Young U.P. Authors Section

Over this last school year, the Upper Peninsula Publishers and Authors Association (UPPAA) held the Dandelion Cottage Short Story Contest with the Upper Peninsula schools. The *U.P. Reader* is proud to publish the first and second place stories from this year's contest. The dandelion icon indicates which stories in this issue are contest winners. There were entries from all around the U.P. and the judges had to declare a tie for the third place. Here is a list of the winners.

1st Place: *The Attack* by **Katie McEachern** of Negaunee

2nd Place: *Welcome to the New Age* by **Emma Locknane** of Gwinn

3rd Place tie: *Elite* by **Anna Laakso** of Republic/Michigamme &

Henry the Kitten by **Sarah Lauzon** of Ironwood

Honorable Mention for *Abducted* by **Sierra Hendrickson** of Negaunee

Katie McEachern is a freshman at Negaunee High School. During her first year, she is active in band, chorus and gymnastics. In her free time Katie enjoys music, writing, drawing, poetry and many other fine arts. She also enjoys adventuring to "cool and unique" places. Additionally, Katie spends time taking pictures with friends, babysitting and doing makeup.

Emma Locknane is a junior at Gwinn High School. She enjoys hobbies such as writing, drawing, knitting, and daydreaming. Her favorite reading genres are science fiction, fantasy, and magical realism. She has many stories of her own she's working on, and often spends her time developing characters and fictional worlds.

Anna Laakso is a sophomore at Republic-Michigamme High School. She is an avid fan of the fantasy genre and seeks it out in her reading and writing choices. Anna is also a talented artist, and her love of fantasy comes through in her many illustrations and drawings.

Sarah Lauzon is an 11 year-old fifth-grader who attends Luther L. Wright K-12 School in Ironwood. She won the 2018 fifth grade U.P. spelling bee. She loves to read and write. She loves cats and Broadway. Her hobbies include playing piano, playing with her cat and swimming.

We hope you enjoy reading the top-ranking stories from these amazing young writers of the U.P. At the end of this section, you'll find an invitation to contribute to this year's contest which closes on December 31st.

The Attack

by Katie McEachern

◆❖◆

I felt him on top of me. I felt his hands move places they should have never been. I reached back, searching for his hand. I felt him ripping off my clothes, his nails scratching my lower back. I squeezed his hand and used whatever horror I had as adrenaline and attempted to throw his hand off me. For a moment his hand was gone, but not for long. He grasped my wrist so tight I couldn't help but let out a small whimper. He was much larger than me and twice as strong. I was helpless below his hands. I was weak and intoxicated. I couldn't fight back. I tried to cry out, I tried to shuffle out from underneath the powerful body on top of me. I grunted and squealed softly, hoping he'd hear the sounds of distress and take pity on me. He didn't. Instead, he leaned his head closer to mine. I felt his breath on the back of my neck and my heart stopped. I heard him speak softly in my ear, telling me not to move or make a sound, that I would be fine, to try to sleep. I felt a tear roll down my face as he placed his hands on me again; they were hot and heavy. I felt them burn holes in my skin as he pressed his body into mine. I screamed pathetically; I made whatever sound I was capable of making, hoping for something loud enough to be heard by anyone but myself and the man I was pinned under. Instead, it came out a pathetic grunt, quickly silenced by his heavy hand when it slammed down over my mouth. I shook my head, hoping to release my face from beneath his hand, hoping to let out another cry for help. I felt his hand leave my mouth for a moment. I prayed it was over, but when I felt his hand smash into the side of my head, I knew. I saw the anger in his eyes and he must have seen the horror in mine during that split second before he placed his hands on me again, one covering my mouth and hiding my sobs as my entire world slipped out of control.

It was the last night of summer. Nineteen days after he attacked me. I sat in bed, wearing only my shorts and a T-shirt, scrolling through social media and seeing everyone's posts about how summer would be missed. Not by me, not in the slightest. In fact, I would give anything if I could make this summer just go away. I slid my finger down the screen and stopped. I looked at the aggravating photo on the phone in front of me. There he was, smiling in the middle of a group of friends at an end-of-summer party. The grip I had on my phone tightened; my hand shook. I brought my fists to my head and tried to bash away the memory of what he had done to me. I slammed my phone onto the bed next to me and stood up angrily, whipping the blanket off my body. I hated seeing him happy. I hated the fact that he was so okay and unaffected by the pain he had caused me. I wanted him to feel the pain I felt, the pain he made me feel. I wanted him to know pain as I knew it because of what he did to me. I hated him. I hated him more than I hated myself for letting him into my room, into my life. I wished hell upon that boy. I wanted him to burn, spiral out of control as I was doing in this moment of anger and had been since he forced himself on me. I wanted revenge; I wanted to make him as horrified, hurt, and helpless he made me. I wanted to break him from the inside of his own mind, exactly as he did to me. At this point, I didn't know what I wanted more, peace or revenge. Revenge would give me peace, knowing that he suffered for what he did to me. I wanted him to suffer, and I wanted to be the one to make him suffer. I wanted him to wake up crying and sweating like I did, and continue to do, every time I dream of that night. I wanted his dreams to be haunted with the image of me, just as mine are haunted by the memory of him. More than I wanted anything, more than I wanted to feel safe again, more than I wanted that sweet taste of liquor or the short pain of a cigarette when it burns your lungs on that first hit that I used to crave so much, more than I had ever wanted anything, I wanted him to feel all the physical, mental, and emotional pain he made me feel, tenfold.

I sat down on the cold leather seats of the Impala and turned the key, listening to the calming purr of the engine starting. I turned up the radio as I watched my younger sister, Summer, walk toward the car. I adjusted the mirror, taking a few moments to look at the tattoo of a rose behind my ear which represented my name as well as my deceased mother, Rosaline. The tattoo was mostly hidden by the long, wavy brown hair my sister and I shared. My hazel eyes looked back at me, eyes that once sought out adventure, but now only sought safety and peace of mind, which have been gone from my life for so long. I put on another quick layer of the stolen red lipstick and looked away from the girl in the mirror.

I heard the car door open and watched as Summer sank into the seat. She had been complaining about high school in the weeks before; this was her first day. We arrived at school and she quickly got out of the car, probably hurrying to talk to all of her freshman friends. I, on the other hand, sat in the car a minute longer. This was going to be hell and I knew it. I had been avoiding nearly everyone since the night of the attack, and nobody knew why. I couldn't tell a soul. They wouldn't understand. They would say it was my own fault because I let him in and took the drinks he gave me, or that I should have expected it. But how can you expect such a horrible thing from a person you thought you could trust? You can't. Instead, everyone assumed I was off on another adventure to Neverland, smoking boxes of stolen cigarettes and ignoring the world like I often did during the hot summer months. This was only half true. I began stealing more cigarettes after the attack. The smell of the smoke reminded me of my mother, reminded me of safety when she held me in her arms. God, I wish I had a cigarette now.

I turned off the car and got out, making sure all the doors were locked and everything I needed for the first day of my last year of high school was in my bag. I walked confidently through the doors of my high school as I always did. I greeted old friends and answered the continuous questions of "Where were you this summer?" with the believable answer of "Adventuring," but in all honesty, I spent my summer with an overwhelming feeling of emptiness. The only rush I got was the rush of vomit after drinking and sobbing the night away.

I kept my eyes up, looking ahead toward my first class. I scanned the hallway, checking for any new faces, when I saw his. I looked into his eyes for the first time since that night. Under my breath I whispered, "No," quiet enough that I wouldn't catch anyone's attention. *This isn't real. It's another flashback*, I thought to myself. I blinked; the black calmed me until I opened my eyes again and saw his face. I saw him walk toward me and I felt my body tense. I saw his eyes look blankly into mine. It was the first time I had looked into his eyes since the night he attacked me, the night he came into my empty house, into my bedroom, my safe place, and made it no longer safe. The night he got me so drunk I couldn't fight him off when he got on top of me and I closed my eyes tightly, begging that when I opened them again he would be gone. He was still there, looking back at me. I almost broke down right there, right in front of him, in front of everyone. Instead, I clenched my jaw, balled my hand into a fist, and turned in the opposite direction. The people around me were like mannequins. The only real things in that hallway were me, him, and the horror and hatred I felt.

I rushed to the bathroom and set my books down on the floor and squeezed the edges of the sink as I looked at the tears falling out of my eyes. I held my fist next to my head for a moment, fighting the urge to shatter the mirror in front of me that showed the frail weak girl I hated seeing. I swung at the solid concrete wall next to the mirror. I felt a jolt run from my knuckles to the center of my upper arm. I wiped the tears away with my sleeve, and looked at the now bruising, slightly busted knuckles on my right hand. I shook my arm quickly and picked up my books. I walked down the hall and arrived at class, sure I had only been a minute.

"Seven minutes late, Miss Rosaline," I heard from the front of the class as I walked to the back and slumped into an empty desk, not saying a word or drawing any attention or concern to myself.

I went along with my day, pretending this morning never happened, pretending this summer never happened. But when I saw him in the halls again, I was again filled with that sharp pain in my heart and horror in my eyes. I walked along, ignoring him and all the things I felt toward him. I couldn't hide, however, when he followed behind me into my fourth hour math class, sitting three seats behind me, or when he sat down at the table behind me at lunch. It was at lunch that the flashbacks began again. My eyes burned red and I could feel the tears beginning to form. I blinked, and I went back to the night he attacked me. I opened my eyes. I was back at school, and so was he. I blinked again. I was pinned down, his eyes full of fire on top

of mine. I opened my eyes. I saw his eyes looking into mine again. I blinked again; I felt the pain in my skull. I opened my eyes; he was gone. I blinked again. Darkness. I opened my eyes. Light. I walked through the crowded hall with a blank stare. The rest of the day, this same thing occurred. Every time I saw him, I'd blink, and it would bring me back to that night.

I waited in the car for Summer to come trotting down the hill to the car. I was never so ready to leave this hell hole. Finally I saw her, walking with a friend I didn't recognize, and behind them, I saw him. I was enraged. He looked at her the same way he looked at me. I felt a fire in my chest. The world slowed almost completely as I watched her approach the car. His eyes stayed on her, and then met mine. The fire in my chest burned brighter. I was filled with the horror from the night this summer as well as overwhelming anger. It took all the power I had to not jump out of the car and dig my fingernails into the eyes that saw my sister and I as prey, but of course I couldn't. I would have to explain to everybody why I gouged out the eyes of a seemingly innocent man, and I couldn't explain to anyone why he wasn't. Especially Summer.

She got into the car and I smiled, though my face was hot with fury. I asked her about her first day; she gave the usual generic answer. "Good." I nodded and hurried away, desperate to keep my sister and me far away from that devil of a boy.

I lay in bed and listened to the silence, only broken by Summer on the phone, talking about all the cute upperclassmen they hadn't seen before. It made me laugh a little, the purity of my little sister. Her laughter, the excitement in her voice. It reminded me so much of my old innocent self. I listened in on her quick goodbye and heard her shuffle into bed. Silence was upon our small house; our grandmother slept quietly. She rarely talked to us; she barely cared about us in all honesty, just as she barely cared about our mother.

When mom was in the hospital, grandma rarely visited. Mom thought it was her own fault, the cancer. I couldn't help but agree. I had asked my mom to stop smoking, warned her that eventually it would kill her. She didn't care, so I stopped caring, too. The only reason Grandma took us in was because of pity. We had no one else. Mom was never married and didn't have any siblings, so no aunts or uncles could take us in. I bet Grandma regretted not having more kids now.

I stared at the ceiling thinking about my day as well as my cursed summer. I closed my eyes, hoping to fall asleep. Instead, another flashback began. This time when I opened my eyes, the horror was far from over. I held it together earlier, but there was no one around to see my break, so I broke. The world around me was silent. The only thing I could hear were the voices in my head. I heard the screams I wish I could have let out that night. I pounded my fists against my head trying to quiet the cries from behind the walls in my mind. My head was on fire and my sanity ran like a child scared of the flames. I was left with nothing but the voices in my head that screamed so loud I could feel my ears vibrate.

I thought of all the ways I could inflict pain on him, but I knew that wasn't an option; he would go to the police, accuse me of being psychotic, and they'd believe it. After all, I have been diagnosed with depression and anxiety—*my mother is dead*—I smoke—I drink, and honestly, with the thoughts I've been having lately, I can't help but think, *Maybe I* am *psychotic.*

Still, I imagined all of the physical pain I felt the night of the attack and the days after, as well as the mental and emotional pain I haven't stopped feeling. The frequent nights when I'm shot back in time to when he shoved himself inside of my weak body while I cried and bled. I imagined every single ounce of my pain inflicted on him, and it brought me the first peace I've had in a long time.

I imagined digging my nails into his body and ripping away at him, splitting the skin beneath my fingertips. The thought made me smile. I imagined how sweet it would be to make him bleed as much as I had when he left me, barely conscious, just lying there. I imagined his blood in my hands. I imagined

the feeling, the warmth, the smell, and horrifyingly enough, the taste.

The space between reality and imagination blurred. I looked at my wrist and saw his in its place. I cautiously walked to my dresser and slowly picked up and inspected the silver metal object in my hand. I smiled as I dragged my knife lightly down my arm. I bit my lip and poked my arm until I felt the skin break underneath the blade. I dragged the blade right, watching as my arm opened revealing a dark red substance, almost like wine. I brought my arm to my lips and sucked the blood out of my arm like wine. I imagined his arm as bloody as mine and laughed; how sweet it would be. I imagined him feeling all this pain I felt. I laughed, I smiled, I sobbed. I watched my blood drip down, I watched my sanity fade away from behind the walls I put up in my mind. I felt myself drifting away.

I was brought back to reality with the sound of a scream. This time, it wasn't my own. It was Summer. I ran out of my room with my pocketknife still in hand. I pushed the door opened with my good arm and looked around my sister's room, searching for the reason for her screams. The room reeked of beer and smoke. Then I saw; it was him. He was in her bed, on top of her. I felt my heart explode with anger as I lunged toward him. I ripped him off of her, swinging my fists at his head. He had destroyed me; I refused to let him destroy her. I swung the knife in his direction, opening a gash in his forearm. He screeched and fell on one knee. He looked up at me slowly. There it was, the anger in his eyes. The same fiery anger I saw the night he pinned me to my own bed just as he did to Summer. This time, I wasn't terrified. I was ready. He kicked my legs out from under me and grabbed my throat with his uninjured arm, pinning me against the floor. I felt the knife fall out of my hand as I began feeling weaker and weaker, losing consciousness from loss of blood and lack of oxygen. I felt the body on top of me fall away as the world around me went black.

I woke up in a somewhat familiar place. I looked around, trying to figure out why exactly I felt at home; this was not my house. I looked around and realized where I was,

Isle Royale 1850

lying in a hospital bed. Summer slept quietly next to me. I looked down, inspecting stitches on my left wrist and a bandage on my right, covering my wrist and knuckles. I tried to sit up, but fell back, cursing at the pain in my head. I lay back down and grabbed Summer's hand. Her eyes shot open; she quickly pushed away my hand, sending a small but sharp pain into my left arm.

"I'm so sorry! Are you okay?" she asked worriedly, finally aware of the situation. She held my arm in front of her, making sure she hadn't hurt me.

"I'm okay, I'm okay," I assured her. I was much more worried about if she was okay and what had happened. Suddenly I felt a wave of anger and horror hit. "Where is he? What did he do to you?" I asked urgently, almost yelling.

"He's in another room. Once he's better they're sending him away," she said reassuringly. I looked at her horrified and anxiously wondered what she went through last night. She saw the look in my eyes. "He came in looking for you; he was drunk and came into my room instead. He got on top of me and covered my mouth, I tried to yell but...." She paused, her eyes starting to water. "I couldn't yell; I couldn't move. I was

so scared, Rose. He hurt me, badly. I fought and fought and was finally able to scream. That's when you came in. I saw your arm, the blood, the knife. You screamed, you ran at him and stabbed him in the arm; he got on top of you and—"

"Stop!" I saw the pain in her eyes and shook my head, I knew what I needed to know. "You're safe now." But she wasn't safe anymore; she would never feel safe again, and it was my fault.

I could have saved her. It took two girls' lives ruined to get this boy in prison, to give him what he deserved, I thought. One of them was my sister, and the first was me. I could have prevented this; I could have let the police handle it instead of trying to handle it myself. I felt so angry at myself. I was too caught up in revenge to protect those around me. I am as bad a person as my attacker, for not saving his next victim. That's when I realized I could have told someone what had happened to me and it would have kept it from happening to someone else, but I was so obsessed with the idea of making him pay myself, I put the people I love in danger. I put Summer in danger. The revenge I was so obsessed with ruined me, and the thing I care about most. It ruined Summer.

Welcome to the New Age

by Emma Locknane

◆❖◆

t'd started as a normal day. Kenta left for school, Chrono lying on the floor in hopeless despair. He'd been in the middle of an existential crisis for days, but Kenta figured it'd blow over like usual. He'd left for school without giving it much thought.

Only when Kenta got home did the trouble start.

He'd walked in to find Lily doing homework. She looked up excitedly when Kenta walked in, but when she saw who it was, she glared.

"Oh, it's just *you*," she grumbled. Lily was a brat to Kenta.

"Who'd you think it was?" Kenta asked, unpacking his books. "The Tooth Fairy?"

"I thought you were Chrono," Lily grumbled. This stopped Kenta.

"He ain't here?"

"He was gone before I got back."

"That's odd...."

"Didn't he have an appointment?"

"Not until eight." Kenta eyed the clock; it was three-thirty....

"Maybe he went grocery shopping." Lily rolled her eyes.

"*Majora* does groceries on Tuesdays," Kenta corrected her condescendingly. "Know where he went?"

"If I knew, I wouldn't have cared when you came!" Lily snipped. Kenta grumbled under his breath. He disliked Lily sometimes.

"Great..." Kenta muttered as a thought formed. "Hey, Contigo!"

"Yes, Master Kenta?" a small voice sounded. A yellow, black-striped cat came trotting down the hall.

"Where's Chrono?" Kenta wondered. Contigo was always on top of things in this house, so Kenta figured he'd be the best source.

"No idea. The master left long ago and made no mention of his destination," Contigo answered. "He seemed rather off today, though...."

"How so?"

"He stared at the ceiling for five hours straight before he departed; wouldn't say a word when I called to him!"

"K...." Kenta realized something was wrong.

"But then around one or so, he just stood up and left. He had a weird look on his face, almost like he was deep in thought," Contigo explained, bordering on a rant. Kenta and Lily both were staring at the cat with bug eyes.

"Like....*thinking* thinking?" Lily asked.

"I'm not a mind reader...but if I had to guess..?" Contigo surmised. Lily and Kenta exchanged a worried glance.

"We've gotta find him!" they exclaimed, shoving their way out the door and slamming it behind them. Contigo stared, befuddled.

"Now they're rushing off in a hurry." He shrugged. "Oh, well. Time for a nap!"

•••

"You know, I just thought!" Lily shouted over the wind. She rode behind Kenta on his hovercycle, flying high above the city with other vehicles and shops below. "A hovercycle is great for speed, but not for spotting Chrono amongst an entire city!"

"Can it, would you?" Kenta hissed. "We're not trying to cover the entire city!"

"Then what *are* we doing?"

"I know Chrono well; he's got several places he goes to when he wants to hide!"

"Guess what? I know him too! What if I have a suggestion?"

"Oh, *what's that*? I can't hear you over the *wind*!" Kenta shouted, feigning deafness.

"Of course you can! I was just—AAH!" Lily shrieked when Kenta accelerated suddenly, ascending to the faster lanes. Lily would've fallen if she weren't holding onto Kenta so tightly.

After several minutes of reckless driving, Kenta landed his hovercycle before a building. A neon-red sign illuminated the words, *The Ballista Bar.*

"The pub?" Lily raised an eyebrow. "Chrono doesn't drink!"

"That's not why he comes here," Kenta retorted. "He hides in the crowds."

"Fine!" Lily groaned, walking toward Kenta.

"Whoa, whoa, whoa! Where you going?" he asked, holding out a hand to block her.

"I'm coming with!"

"No, you're not. Read the sign!" Kenta pointed to a sign on the wall.

Under 18 NOT ALLOWED!

Lily frowned. "So what am I expected to do?"

"Wait here," Kenta told her, walking inside. Lily glared after him.

"Sure, I'll just *stay here*! Not like I could be useful, or anything!" she huffed, but then spotted something across the street. "Hey... is that Fred?"

•••

Kenta strode inside, met by cheers and jeers. He received some shifty stares, returning the gesture. Patrons quickly diverted their attention from him after noting he was a fellow tough character.

Maintaining such composure, Kenta sauntered up to the bar counter, taking a seat beside a hungover woman. The bartender turned round, immediately recognizing Kenta.

"Hey, kid!" the man hollered, his big feet thumping as he approached. "What can I get ya?"

"How about some info?" Kenta queried, leaning his elbows on the counter. The bartender blinked in surprise.

"I'll see what I can do. What's on yer mind?"

"Seen Chrono lately? Within the past few hours?"

"Chrono? Nah, haven't seen him in ages!" the bartender answered. "Why?"

"He disappeared earlier," Kenta replied, running his finger along the counter.

"I see. Might check Fight Club," the bartender suggested. "Lots of people go there to blow off steam."

"That's next," Kenta stood up. "Thanks, anyway."

"No problem! Hope you find your dad!" the bartender called after him. Kenta shot him a look.

"Chrono's not my dad."

"Might as well be. Good luck!"

Kenta sighed, walking out the door. He trotted over to his hovercycle, halting when he saw Lily. She was leaning back against the handlebars, a paper tray in her hands.

"What are you eating?" Kenta asked.

"Sweet potato fries. I got them over there!" Lily pointed across the street where a scruffy old man was manning a stand. "It's Ol' Fred!"

"Fred?" Kenta repeated, confused.

"You don't know Fred?"

"Nope."

"How do you not know *Fred*?"

"I think the better question is how *you* know him!" Kenta shot Lily a harsh stare.

"When Chrono used to drop me off at morning class, we'd stop by Fred's stand in the morning!" Lily explained irritably. "He's got the best sweet potato fries!"

"So you complain about being useless, yet you go buy fries?" Kenta queried.

"Please, I'm not stupid! I asked if he'd seen Chrono," Lily answered. "Nothin'. How'd your expedition go?"

"Not at the bar," Kenta sighed. Lily caught the look in his eyes.

"Fight Club's next?"

"Yep."

•••

Kenta and Lily pulled into the junkyard, a sign illuminating the words *"FIGHT CLUB."* The dim lighting of old vehicles gave off an intimidating atmosphere, but Kenta and Lily had been here enough not to worry.

Once more, Kenta put on his thug stance. The two passed through the crowd watching the current fight. Though the duel was very interesting, the two were low-ranking members on the scoreboard, so Kenta didn't devote attention. He walked up to the burly guard standing near the entrance behind the bleachers.

"Yo, Rufus!" Kenta said. The lizard-faced guard grumbled as he turned his head. A forked tongue flicked through his lips. "Chembra around?"

"What's it to you, gangrene?" Rufus growled throatily, glancing at Kenta's green hair.

"Gotta speak with him."

"What for?"

"Info."

"About?"

"Can I just see him?" Kenta snapped.

Rufus folded his scaly limbs.

"Not just anybody can talk to the champ!" he grumbled.

"I know. I won't be long." Kenta stared back at the dragon of a man. Rufus narrowed his beady eyes, lips curling into a snarl.

"Only because you're Chrono's kid!" he chuffed. "He's in the back preppin' for a match. With the rate it's been goin', though, he could take probably take a nap!"

"Thanks," Kenta quipped, continuing on. "You've always been my favorite!"

"Save it," Rufus snarled back. "Kids...."

Kenta and Lily reached the infirmary, where fighters also prepared for matches. Despite the large number of combatants, it didn't take long to find the Fight Club champion. His black scales, white hair, and vibrant frills stood out.

"Hey, Chembra!" Kenta called. The draker turned his head, eyes lighting up when he saw Kenta.

"Yo! Looky-who?" Chembra chirruped, tufted tail curling with excitement. "How're you?"

"Got somethin' to ask ya." Kenta cut straight to the chase.

"Oh, you do?" Chembra rumbled, the frills on his neck shuffling inquisitively.

"I'm looking for Chrono. Ya seen him?" Kenta queried.

"Not around here."

"Where *did* you see him?" Lily demanded. When Chembra went to respond, she continued, "I know that devious look; all drakers have it when they're hiding something! You know more!"

Chembra blinked twice, impressed.

"All right, I'll talk," Chembra sighed. "I was on my way here earlier, and I saw him ride by on that motorcycle of his. Thing's practically an antique!"

"Where'd you see him?" Lily frowned.

"I'd just left *Anaro's Mexican*; saw him heading northeast!"

"Anything else?"

"Nope. That's it. He went right on by, didn't even wave!" Chembra rolled his eyes. "So rude. I'd waved to him, and everything!"

"Thanks," Kenta stated.

"No problem!" Chembra answered. "That fight done yet? Ricky's up next; I want to know if it's his turn!"

"Nope; still at it!" Kenta informed him. "Catch ya later!"

"Sure thing!" Chembra smiled, waving. "Good luck out there. Don't get run over! Roads are dangerous!"

•••

Kenta and Lily spent the evening scouring DC. They checked everywhere he'd usually be—the library, Scientists' Corner, even the Cat Park. Still, Chrono remained elusive. It had Kenta worried.

"I don't get it!" Kenta stated. He and Lily were in the Cat Park, the hovercycle parked nearby. Lily was watching with an aloof expression. "We've looked everywhere! Where is he?"

"Dunno. DC's huge!" Lily stated. "But if we haven't found him yet, we're probably not going to find him ourselves. I say we file a report!"

Kenta huffed.

"You're kidding, right? If Majora finds out, she'll kill us!"

"You got a better plan? We can't scour the entire city alone!"

"Lily, if we file a report, Majora *will* know!" Kenta tried to reason with her. He didn't want to face the wrath of Chrono's mother. "And you know how she is! She'll flip and ground us for the rest of our *lives*!"

"Whatever. I'm going!" Lily rose, turning and walking away. Kenta glared after her.

"Fine! Don't expect *me* to give you a ride home!"

"Whatever, Seaweed-Head!"

Kenta rolled his eyes, leaning against his bike with a sigh. Truth be told, he *didn't* have a plan for finding Chrono. If he wasn't in any of his usual places, then Kenta didn't know where he'd gone. Chrono wasn't usually this hard to find; it was very uncharacteristic of him.

Suddenly, realization slapped Kenta right across the face. How could he have been so dumb? To think he'd wasted all this time.

"Why didn't I just call him?" Kenta chastised himself. "How did I not think of it earlier?"

Rolling his eyes, Kenta scrolled through his contacts until he found Chrono's name. He got great satisfaction knowing Lily probably hadn't thought of this.

There was the automated sound of a ringing phone—Chrono used an old-fashioned smartphone despite the existence of newer technology—but finally, someone picked up.

"H-hello?" an old, withered voice picked up. Taken aback, the higher pitch immediately told Kenta that it wasn't Chrono.

"Sorry! Wrong number!" Kenta answered, frantically hanging up. He then paused when he realized he couldn't possibly be mistaken; that was the contact he'd put in for Chrono's phone! He'd used it just the other day and it'd worked, so it couldn't be a mistake! If that was true, why did an old lady answer *Chrono's* phone? Kenta called again.

"Hello? Is anyone there?" the elderly voice rasped again.

"Hi! Uhh...I'm looking to speak to Chrono Salvage?" Kenta asked, still trying to wrap his head around what was going on.

"Chrono...I'm afraid I'm not sure who that is!" the old woman answered. "Could you describe them?"

"Pale lavender hair, magenta eyes, lots of scars on his face," Kenta explained.

Silence.

"He's got a metal arm," Kenta added.

"Oh! Why, yes! I've seen him! Such a nice young man!" The old woman finally gave some well-needed answers. "In fact, he's here now!"

"Where?" Kenta demanded, finally getting a lead.

"Room 206, floor three!"

"What *building*?"

"The Blue Evans Retirement Home."

What the heck is he doing there, retiring? Kenta asked himself. He's only forty!

"And...where *is* that?" Kenta queried.

"Quadrant Three, two roads inland from Engelman Industries, on the left!" the lady answered. "It's a brick building, with a big pink sign on the roof; can't miss it!"

"All right, thanks," Kenta responded.

"No problem! Are you a friend?" the woman queried.

"You could say that—"

"Wonderful! Well, I'll just tell him you're coming," the woman chimed merrily.

"No, no! Wait a minute; don't tell him I—!" Kenta blurted, but it was too late. The woman had already hung up the phone. "Agh, great...."

Kenta jumped onto his hovercycle and set off as fast as possible. He had to get to the retirement home before Chrono could escape; Kenta would lose the trail if he got too far ahead. The jitakarai was a fickle creature in such circumstances; one minute he'd decide he wanted to be found, but the second he realized he was being tracked he'd disappear. Usually he could be found with relative ease, but Kenta could sense today was different....

•••

Kenta careened into the parking lot, throwing his bike into park and charging inside. He barged through the doors, shoving up to the receptionist.

"I need to find Room 206!" he shouted. The receptionist stared up at him with bored eyes, slowly putting on glasses.

"What floor?" she asked blandly, raising an eyebrow.

"Three!"

"Go up the elevator; tenth room on the right, down the hall."

"Thanks!" Kenta took off, jumping in the elevator and smashing the button. As the elevator shifted, Kenta hoped Chrono hadn't gotten away yet....

The elevator doors opened, and Kenta sprinted down the hall until he came to 206. Skidding to a halt, he battered on the door.

"Who is it?" a shriveled voice asked.

"The person who called looking for Chrono Salvage," Kenta answered, hoping the old lady didn't have dementia or anything....

To his relief, someone actually answered. A small, frail old lady with a walker stood in the doorway, looking Kenta up and down. She smiled a very slow, welcoming grin.

"Ah! So you found us, then!" she said. "Come in!"

The old woman hobbled back into the room, and Kenta followed. He entered a small, dimly lit room with beige walls and maroon carpeting. There were several chairs arranged in a circle, all but two filled with elderly. Chrono was nowhere to be seen.

"Hey, where'd he go?" Kenta asked, beginning to feel irritated. The old people didn't answer, just kept staring at Kenta.

"A youngster?" an old docani asked, barely looking up from her knitting. Her big, bushy tail twitched in agitation while one of her long, almost elephant-like ears cocked with query. "We never get those 'round here!"

"You look a lot like my late husband," another woman stated, a faraway look in her eyes. "All tough and the like! He was a drug lord...and a hitman.... Ah, but I loved him!"

"Do you have my Metamucil?" an elderly vultasian woman asked, a bat-like ear raised in query.

Kenta cringed.

"Girls, girls!" the woman with the walker berated, gesturing with her hands. "Behave yourselves! We're trying to help this young man find his friend, not comment on the state of DC's youth!"

Thank you! Kenta thought.

"Come, young man! Take a seat," the woman insisted, gesturing to the last chair she pushed into the center of the circle. Kenta acquiesced as a form of respecting his elders.

"So, Chrono *was* here, right?" he asked.

"Mm-hm! Just as you described him!" the woman said.

"So pleasant!" the cloudy-eyed woman cooed.

"Okay. But where is he *now*?" Kenta persisted.

"Up and left us!" the docani snapped. "Said he had somethin' to attend to!"

"Of course he did..." Kenta groused. "Know where he went?"

"No!" the docani hissed, narrowing her eyes. "He didn't tell us! Not that it's our business."

"K...." Kenta relented, knowing he had a new trail, now. "Thanks anyway."

"Siddown, boy! We're not done with ya!" she barked, her tone so vicious that Kenta didn't argue for a second. The docani looked to the woman with the walker expectantly.

"Your friend was quite downcast when he came," the woman spoke with concern.

"What do you mean?" Kenta queried, listening.

"Oh, the poor thing! He looked like something the cat dragged in!" the vultasian exclaimed.

"Was he hurt?"

"No, not physically!" the vultasian answered. "He looked a little dead inside, perhaps!"

"Like a shell with no hermit crab," the cloudy-eyed woman added eerily.

"So...he's depressed?" Kenta guessed.

"Isn't that what 'downcast' means?" the docani snarked with a tone like sandpaper. Kenta would never forget her scowl...

"He was, actually," the walker lady replied. "See, when we asked him why he was here, he said he'd come seeking...advice!"

"I told him to invest in some orthopedic shoes!" the vultasian piped up.

"Advice? That's odd..." Kenta murmured, realizing the severity of the problem....

"He said he was trying to reconnect with someone, but wasn't sure how. Apparently everything he'd tried hadn't worked, so he'd come to see if we had any input," the walker lady elucidated. "So we told him!"

"Told him what?" Kenta asked, confused where this was going.

"Our stories." The docani didn't look up from her knitting.

"I told him about my niece!" the vultasian said. A glimmer of glee passed over her eyes. "Would you like to hear it?"

"Maybe another time. Why did you tell him stories?" Kenta tried to reason.

"What else are we gonna do? Dance a jig?" The docani raised a sarcastic eyebrow. "Ha! We're way beyond that, son! Our lips are the only things that still work!"

"But who does he have this issue with?" Kenta queried, beginning to lose patience.

"Didn't say. And we didn't ask!" the docani chuffed. "It wasn't something he wanted to disclose, and we respected that!"

"We were just glad for a visitor!" the walker lady said. "We don't get many guests; we were happy to have someone listen to us for a while!"

"He was actually interested when I told him how I finally got my daughter to visit me!" the cloudy-eyed woman added. "Hanging on every word, absorbing every detail like a little sponge!"

"Mm-hm! Francine seemed to be the one he focused on the most!" the walker lady pointed out. "I mean, he listened to *all* of us without fail, but that story seemed to *really* snag his attention!"

"Until you wrecked it!" the docani snapped.

"Go on," Kenta prompted softly.

"You called him, and he went on the fritz!" The docani waved her pair of hands that wasn't busy knitting. "He couldn't even bear to answer the darn thing, he was so distraught! Ruthie had to answer, instead!"

"Oh, I felt so bad!" the walker lady, Ruthie, sighed. "He looked terrified!"

"Why would he be scared to answer his own phone?" Kenta wondered aloud, mostly to himself.

"Dunno; you tell us!" The docani gave Kenta a warning glare. "You givin' him a reason?"

"I don't know. He's never done this before. Did he ask you anything specific?" Kenta asked, looking to Ruthie.

"No, but he did say something rather odd," Ruthie answered. "Something about not wanting to be seen in such a state."

"He was that upset? You must have some idea *why!*" Kenta exclaimed.

"Like we said, he looked pretty messed up walkin' in!" the docani stated. "Almost as if he were in a state of despair. When we started talkin' to him, he lit up like we were *saints*, or somethin'!"

"I have to find him. Who knows what sort of trouble he's gotten himself into...?" Kenta sighed, rising from the chair. "Thank you for your time. Uh...do you know anyone who might know where he went?"

"Belle knows," a small voice peeped from the window. A small old lady in a wheelchair sat hunched by the window, her long white hair hanging in ghostly wisps over her face.

"Where is she, then?" Kenta queried.

"Belle is right here," the old woman stated.

"She speaks in the third person!" Ruthie whispered. "Just go with it!"

"Ah..." Kenta understood. "And...what did Belle see?"

"She saw through the window; after Ruthie told him you were coming, he thanked us for our time and left in a hurry." Belle continued staring. "Belle saw him ride off on a motorcycle."

"I see. You sure he headed in that direction?" Kenta asked for clarification.

Soo Railroad Bridge Collapse Engine Recovery - Oct 1941

"Yes; off toward the northeast. Belle thinks it's possible you may find him near the docks." Belle turned her head slowly, giving Kenta a queer stare through her milky eyes.

"Thank you. If there's nothing else you have to tell me, I have to go," Kenta told the ladies.

With that, Kenta slowly made his way back to the parking lot. He mounted his hover-cycle, started the engine, and rocketed full speed for the docks.

•••

Kenta raced through the streets of DC, his mind fixated on finding Chrono. Kenta's thoughts were aimed at the docks, and where Chrono might be hiding. He was tough to find when he didn't want to be found, but he had some habits that never failed. Kenta knew he was particularly drawn to old structures. In quadrant two, most of the old docks were located on the northwest region. If Kenta had to guess, he figured that's where Chrono would be.

As Kenta raced along, he came upon a familiar sight. Grinding to a halt, he noticed a small shack placed a few meters from an abandoned ore dock. Reading the sign, Kenta vaguely recognized it.

The Koffee Kat

Kenta recalled this building. When Kenta was younger, likely in middle-school, Chrono would sometimes return with scones from here. The logo of the brown cat in a coffee cup had always been a prominent symbol in his mind; this place had the best scones....

Running over to the ore dock, Kenta stopped as he came across a motorcycle parked nearby.

It was definitely Chrono's, possessing wheels worn from years of use. Frowning, Kenta proceeded onto the dock, running down the length until he spotted a figure huddled in a thick black coat near the end.

It was Chrono.

Kenta cautiously stepped forward. He didn't know if Chrono noticed him or not, and he didn't want to startle him lest he disappear again. Kenta continued until he was right behind the jitakarai.

"Chrono."

It took a moment before Chrono slowly turned his head. His wispy lavender hair hung over his eyes, so there was no telling what he was thinking.

"You know I've been looking for you all day?" Kenta began, sitting down.

"Figured," Chrono answered emotionlessly.

"Why'd you run off? You know you had an appointment?" Kenta asked, clueless as to what instigated the jitakarai to disappear.

"I already canceled it."

"Why?" Kenta wondered.

Chrono shrugged. "Mm."

"Hey, you set me on this *adventure* knowing I'd have to track you down, and that's all you can say?"

"I guess."

"Don't give me that! I'm already getting in trouble for leaving Lily by herself and talking to a bunch of strange old ladies, and you won't give me a reason? Are you *trying* to get me grounded? 'Cuz you sure done me in this time!" Kenta shouted, unable to be calm any longer.

"No, the retirement home thing is on me," Chrono sighed. "And that wasn't my intention. That was collateral that only crossed my mind afterwards."

"Why did you go there in the first place?" Kenta demanded to know.

"Advice."

"Yeah. I got that. Tell me *why*."

Chrono was silent, sighing through his nose. He continued staring somberly into the distance, hair blowing in his face. Finally, however, the slightest glimmer of emotion swirled across his irises.

"I remember the first time I showed you the lab," Chrono began. Kenta wasn't sure where he was going, but he let Chrono speak. "You were...thirteen, maybe twelve and a half.

You'd been begging to see it for weeks, and finally I gave in."

Kenta remained silent, remembering how many times he tried to break into that lab. Every time he'd gotten caught by some sort of security measure, however.

"You were so excited," Chrono continued. "I remember...your face just lit up when you saw it."

Kenta listened quietly, recalling such.

"It was like a kid in a candy store; you were so fascinated by everything," Chrono went on, eyes still focused off into the distance. "Jerry, especially. You couldn't get enough of him."

Kenta's memory of that day passed before his eyes. He'd always wondered what that big cage out back housed, and he finally got to see it. Initially, he was frightened of the mutant flytrap, as it was taller than the house. However, after Chrono assured him it was friendly, he'd tentatively wandered forth to pet it. Nowadays, Kenta and the giant plant were good buddies.

"I also...remember when you first got your hovercycle." A flicker of nostalgia twirled across Chrono's expression.

"Yeah. It was black with green highlights. We still have it stored away in the garage," Kenta replied, thinking back to the first time he had crashed it. He couldn't count the times Chrono had had to fix it.

"I know; I saw it earlier," Chrono responded.

"You had it out recently?" Kenta wondered.

"Yeah."

"Why? Was it rusty?" Kenta queried.

"No. Those things never rust."

"Right. Why'd you have it out?"

"Bit of maintenance."

"Think she'll run after crashing in the lake?"

"Of course she'll run. A few spare parts ought to do nicely."

"You know...I was thinking of...letting Lily have it. When she's ready, that is. Well, only if she doesn't get me *grounded*!"

"I had a similar thought."

"Little brat. She'd probably be a pro her first time! She'd just speed off as if she owned the road!" Kenta shook his head.

"Be nice; a hovercycle's a far cry from that moped of hers!" Chrono chastised him. "And she's not a brat!"

"Yes *she is*! She acts like an angel toward *you*, but she's a little monster to me! She always has some sassy remark!" Kenta snapped.

Chrono sighed. "Well...yes! She usually does, and she needs to work on that!" he stated. "But she's still your sister! Adopted, sure, but family nonetheless! So I don't want to hear you calling her a monster! You're lucky to have her."

Kenta stopped. He knew Chrono wasn't so fortunate. He'd lost both his sisters, and Kenta knew the jitakarai still blamed himself for them.

"I know, but she's still mean...!" he pointed out.

"I'll get on her case later. But just because she's mean to you doesn't give you license to mistreat her!" Chrono chuffed. "Be a good brother!"

"Hey, she left *me*! I didn't twist her arm," Kenta retorted.

"I'm not saying you did."

Kenta gave him a certain face, frustrated that he couldn't dispute that.

There was another long silence; the stars barely visible in the green-blue sky. Seagulls squawked down by the docks against the ambiance of Navy ships scrolling through the harbor. Music was faintly heard from the Koffee Kat's interior. Once again, Chrono fell quiet.

Kenta sighed.

"With Alex and Jared in college, they ain't got time for me, you know? I miss 'em. Wish they'd at least stop by now and then. Alex's all about the island these days, and Jared has all this homework...."

"That happens with age and experience; such loneliness."

"You saying you're lonely?" Kenta asked, surprised. "I mean, with five people in the house, I'd think you'd be sick of people."

"You'd think."

"How are you lonely, Chrono?" Kenta wondered, shocked. Chrono paused, a forlorn look on his face.

"I'm still important to you, right?" he queried sadly.

Kenta nearly choked on his scone, whipping his head toward Chrono with wide, bewildered eyes.

"Of course! You raised me, took me in when no one else wanted a thieving child of a drug abuser, and turned my life around! I...maybe haven't done much to repay you...but Chrono...surely you realize..."

Chrono chuffed in a manner similar to that of a housecat.

"I suppose it's silly of me. Gettin' senile early, I guess!" he interjected, trying to brush off his words.

"No, I'm serious. You *are* important to me, Chrono. I just haven't—I haven't had the time, no—that's not...."

"I get it. Homework. High school. Tough years, I can attest."

"It doesn't excuse how I never showed you appreciation! I know I don't always take your plights as seriously as I should...but I still care! Everyone's busy; everyone has homework, but it doesn't mean they can ignore everyone! I just wish...."

Chrono's gaze remained clouded.

Kenta hated that face. He'd seen it too often to ignore it now.

Kenta grabbed Chrono and yanked him close. This startled the jitakarai, who moved to shove Kenta away, but never completed the action.

Kenta hugged him tighter, ensuring the jitakarai wouldn't escape him ever again.

"Just because you're not my actual dad doesn't mean I don't consider you one," Kenta whispered, voice trembling. This finally broke Chrono, who was reduced to a sobbing, shaking mess in Kenta's arms. He buried his face into Kenta's shoulder, emotion finally overtaking him.

They stayed like that for a while, mentor and apprentice, father and son. Finally, at least for a moment as the stars twinkled down on them, everything seemed right with the world.

"Come on, then," Kenta said, finally releasing Chrono and getting to his feet. "Let's go home."

Young Writers Encouraged to Submit to 2018 Dandelion Cottage Short Story Contest.

Contest Rules
- Schools may nominate up to two short stories to represent their school.
- Home-schooled students may submit stories through their local school.
- Maximum length: 5,000 words.
- Authors must attend or be home-schooled in an Upper Peninsula School District.
- Teachers, parents, and others may offer suggestions and comments, but all writing must be the work of the author. In the real literary world, editors will offer suggestions. **This is to be a learning experience.**
- Teachers, parents, and others may point out spelling and grammatical errors on the finished manuscript, but the author is responsible for understanding and correcting all errors. **This is to be a learning experience.** In the real literary world, copyeditors will be correcting these errors. We expect polished submissions.

- Short stories must be submitted electronically in MS Word or PDF format prior to December 31st of the current calendar year to be considered in that contest year.
- Authors will retain the copyright to their work, but UPPAA reserves first publishing rights for eighteen months after submission. Selected works may also appear in a "Best of U.P. Reader" edition to mark our 10th anniversary.

Recognition
- First place winner will receive $250.
- Second place winner will receive $100.
- Third place winner will receive $50.
- Winning school will receive a trophy for display during the coming year.

T. Kilgore Splake

Brautigan Creek Magic

hiking forest path
hearing river sounds
currents ebbing and
flowing
running over and around
rocks
soft musical melody
smelling earth
rotten leaves acrid stink
dark forest cranny
not touched by sun
poet drawn to water
primal sensation
of returning to embryo
safe amniotic home
walking creek banks
feeling magic spirit
deeper wilderness trek
poet seeking
serious creative voice
brautigan creek beginning

Another Morning

exploding alarm clock
waking weary brain
lying in bed
eyes slowly focusing
staring at ceiling tiles
rigid arthritic bones
feeling like rigor mortis
growing coffee thirst
bladder needing relief
dull morning light
filtering through drapes
blank page waiting
graying poet's pen
elusive dame muse
rat bastard time
determined creative foes
all too soon
death stealing vision
denying hemingway
depression
papa's 12 gauge solution
or leonard cohen
telling lord he's ready
"kill the flame
make it darker"
soon outside myself
pressing imagination
making words sing

T. Kilgore Splake ("the cliffs dancer") lives in a tamarack location old mining row house in the ghost copper mining village of Calumet in Michigan's Upper Peninsula. His most recent book *depot* is a modest history of the old railroad station located in Calumet. Splake has several photographs and poems in the new issue of *Clutch* (Street Corner Press, Sister Bay, Wisconsin). In addition, Splake is awaiting the arrival of two new chapbooks: *entropy* and *world by myself.*

Bottom Feeder

by Aric Sundquist

Fredrick Morrison sat hunched over his drawing. The picture was inspired from a book Miss Shepherd had just finished reading to her third-grade class, a book he had read three times before called *Journey to the Center of the Earth* by Jules Verne.

Fredrick loved the part about the sea serpents the best. When those three spelunkers were stranded on a raft and had to paddle to shore while fending off gigantic flesh-eating plesiosaurs. But then his teacher had to go and ruin it.

This is what happened.

Miss Shepherd folded up her book, set it in her lap, and regarded her students one by one. She said there were no such things as sea serpents, especially ones that ate humans, and that those huge fish only wanted to sneak a peek at the scientists and play with them in the water. They were nice, curious dinosaurs.

Fredrick glanced around and noticed the same perplexed look melting onto the faces of just about everyone else in the room, except maybe the girls, who probably liked nice sea serpents better. So he fumed and rocked dangerously in his seat, and then his hand rocketed up, knocking his pencil onto the floor.

Miss Shepherd's lazy brown eyes drifted from the fallen pencil to Fredrick's face. She exhaled loudly through her nose, and then opened up to her bookmarked page.

Fredrick wiggled his fingers, his wrist, his whole arm. He was almost standing. She still ignored him and poured over the text. He waved both hands as if landing an airplane. But she had already found her spot and resumed reading.

Miss Shepherd soon finished the book and informed her class she would be reading *The Hobbit* by J. R. R. Tolkien next week. Fredrick was happy when he heard this, but only for a moment. He knew the goblins and dwarves and the great dragon Smaug would all be pals by the end. What fun was that?

He decided to get even with his teacher.

He began drawing a picture from the Jules Verne book, a project requested by Miss Shepherd. The assignment was to draw a single scene that they liked the most.

In late August, during the first week of school, Miss Shepherd had rationed off fifteen packages of fresh Crayola crayons. The kids couldn't wait to put the pretty colors to paper. But she had taken out all the black and purple crayons from each pack, broken them in half, and thrown them in the garbage. She didn't like those colors because they were too dark, even though purple would have made a better underground sky than any other color. So he had to improvise.

Fredrick first began by coloring the sky a dark orange with spots of red. His teacher said that it looked like the leaves outside and the drawing so far was very pretty. He waited until she left. Next came the water, light blue, and then a brown raft, unoccupied, and the final details of his work. He glanced up and saw her coming back around, patting Chrissy Jordan on the shoulder, smiling at her best student. And then his teacher regarded him. Their eyes met. He was up to something. And she knew it.

"Can I see your drawing, Freddy?" she asked, kneeling down and pushing her thick glasses farther up her nose. "I really like what you did with the sky. Red and orange are good colors, don't you think?"

"I'm not done yet," he said politely, twisting his neck and spreading his arms around the drawing. "I want to show you it when it's all done."

She laughed. "I know, sweetie. But I want to see what else you've done. Can I see?"

"Well—"

She tugged on the edge of the drawing, pulled hard with long fingers and nails with layers of red nail polish that had started to peel on the edges. The top corner of the drawing began to tear. If he didn't let go, she would rip it in half.

"Let me see," she said.

He let her have the drawing. She scooped it up and held it to the light.

Fredrick didn't see her face. Didn't have to. The silence was long enough to tell him she disapproved. He stared at his red crayon, twisted it around and around in his fingers.

In the picture, the three men were swimming in the clutches of the blue waves. Underneath, a red serpent with spiky fins was sliding up from its ocean bed, all razor teeth and with a hungry smile. It was going to feast on the scientists.

"Hmmm," she said, giving him a wary look. "This doesn't happen in the book."

"I know, but—"

"I don't think I can post this up on the board with the others."

She folded the drawing in half, then strutted quickly back to her desk and stuck it in her desk drawer.

Later that day, as he was getting ready to go home, pulling on his boots and jacket in the cloakroom (a stupid name, he always thought, since nobody wears cloaks anymore), he saw her pull out his drawing and stare at it. He crept up closer and watched through the crack in the door, saw her shake her head in disgust and rip up his drawing, then throw the pieces into the wastebasket.

•••

The next day, Miss Shepherd's third grade class had an aquarium, donated from a local pet store that had gone out of business. The whole class was in a frenzy when they saw the huge twenty-gallon tank. A bubbler purred and little bubbles drifted to the top. On the bottom were blue pebbles, a few tumbled stones and some plastic weeds. They swayed gently from the resonance of the filtration system.

"Tomorrow we'll be getting fifteen fish from the pet store for our new tank," Miss Shepherd said. "Fifteen fish. That's one for each of you! Now, tomorrow I want everybody to pick out an extra special fish and take care of it. Watch it grow." She waved a finger in the air. "Think of a name tonight."

The whole class was in an uproar.

Reading time was right after lunch. Fredrick had a book that he kept secret from his teacher, stashed under all his textbooks and folders, called *The World's Scariest Ghost Stories*. On the cover, an apparition drifted across an oak floor, holding her severed head cupped in her arm. Her name was Marie Antoinette. The book was full of scary ghost stories and legends that were all true. His favorite, "The Brown Lady of Raynham Hall," was one of the first apparitions caught on camera in the 1940s—a misty, transparent woman in a flowing robe descending a staircase in London. The picture was the best ghost picture ever. It baffled scientists and skeptics, and when Fredrick first looked at it, he became a believer.

He stashed his book inside *Jack and the Beanstalk* because the cover was so big. He had just found a spot in the farthest corner, near the chalkboard, and opened up his hidden book, when Miss Shepherd walked over to him and knelt down.

"You know, Freddy," she said, "you should really sit with your classmates."

He nodded and stood up.

"Just don't tell any more spooky stories," she continued. "You scared poor Claudia half to death. Okay?"

"Yes, Miss Shepherd."

"So, you're reading *Jack and the Beanstalk* again?" She reached out and felt the hard cover with her fingertips. "Freddy," she pleaded, "I really want you to read something you haven't read before. Here—" She grabbed the book out of his hands before he could say a word, and the hidden book slipped to the floor.

Miss Shepherd regarded the book for a moment, picked it up, and glanced at the front cover. "This isn't a book from my library," she said. "Is it yours?"

"Yes, Miss Shepherd."

"It looks disgusting. But you like that stuff, don't you? You like that sick stuff, right?"

He didn't answer. She gave him the book back, shook her head, and went around to her students, laughing and talking about the importance of reading the proper books.

Freddy watched all her kids beam at her and brandish their books, spellbound.

And, of course, she approved of every one.

•••

It was Friday morning when they arrived and the tank was full of fish that bobbed and weaved and looked pretty in the glossy water. Miss Shepherd summoned them all up close and told them which kind of fish they were.

There were six little fish called tetras; four of them were blue and red, and two were pure white; there were two yellow goldfish and two white goldfish, four ghost-fish you could see right through—spine and all, and an ugly fish with whiskers and brown spots that had a round mouth stuck to the glass. Miss Shepherd said that the suckerfish was a bottom feeder and helped clean the tank, helped balance out the *eco-system*—a word she repeated three times, slowly. The suckerfish had to be in there or else all the fish would get tummy-aches from the bad water.

That's how she said it: *tummy-aches*.

She had her students sit down at their desks and called them up, one at a time.

Fredrick watched each student walk up, tap the glass, choose one, and then announce a name to Miss Shepherd, who wrote everything down on a red card.

Blue Man, Shadow, Daisy.

The names were sometimes funny, too. Sammy called his goldfish Luke Skywalker, because he had just seen *Return of the Jedi* at the theater, and Claudia called her little tetra Moby Dick. Since some of the fish were the same kind, they had to find characteristics or flaws that made them unique. Some had larger mouths or were more red than blue; some of the ghost fish were larger while others had smaller fins.

Fredrick tapped his feet and waited for his turn. He wanted a ghost fish. He liked how they swam, like polished glass slipping through the water, and he liked how they floated like an apparition, hardly noticed at all. He couldn't wait. He would call his fish Mr. Skeleton. It was a good name.

But then, as each kid went up, the supply dwindled, until there was only one ghost fish left.

And then it, too, was picked.

Fredrick was last and there were no ghost fish left, not even any tetras or goldfish. So when his teacher finally called his name, he slipped out of his seat, dragged his feet up, and regarded his ugly fish on the bottom. The class laughed behind him because his fish was so ugly and never swam. It just slipped along the bottom and stuck to things, minding its own business. There was a slight discoloration around the gills, faint reddish spots. He wondered if the fish was sick, or perhaps it was some sort of infection that would pass to the other fish in the aquarium.

"What do you want to name your fish?" Miss Shepherd asked.

He had to think of a name, and quick. It had two long whiskers, so he said, quite spontaneously, "Catfish Bob."

The class roared in laughter a second time. His fish was stupid and so was the name he had picked.

"The good thing about your fish is that you never have to feed him," Miss Shepherd said. "He's a bottom feeder and eats algae and the droppings of all the other fish."

The class roared with laughter a third time. The loudest time.

Freddy sat down in his seat. His face felt like it was burning up.

"And now I'll show you all *my* fish," Miss Shepherd said, walking to her desk and pulling out a baggy full of water.

Whispers went around, in shock, in excitement, in anticipation of one last fish that was hidden from them. Fredrick was curious, too, and watched her show her fish. It was beautiful, with a long tail and flowing fins. Miss Shepherd said it was a shark of some sort, and named it Angel.

She showed it to each of her students. Then she opened the baggy and dumped it inside the tank.

It flowed instead of swam.

•••

That day, at recess, Fredrick was hanging upside down on the monkey bars, pretending to be a bat sleeping in a cave, when he felt a thump against his stomach. He opened his eyes.

Dale Wright was thin as a willow leaf. "Hey, Batman," he said. "Nap time's over." He laughed, more of a nasal wheeze than anything.

Dale's best friend, Chad McDeever, was there also. Every time Freddy saw him, he always thought of a bullfrog.

Dale and Chad weren't nasty bullies or anything, but they weren't altogether nice, either. Sometimes they just got bored and wanted to mess around with people, preferably victims who never fought back.

"So, Freddy," Dale continued, slipping his hands in his pockets and rocking on the balls of his feet. "Why'd you call your fish such a stupid name?"

Freddy pulled himself up and jumped down. "I don't know," he said. "I don't think it's *that* stupid."

"What!" Chad interrupted. "Catfish Bob is a stupid-ass name! Come on! Hey, wait a minute." He shouldered Dale. "Doesn't Freddy kind of look like his fish? When his lip goes up like that. You like eating fish shit, too? Huh?"

Freddy clenched his mouth shut.

"Hey, Betty!" Chad yelled, sticking his head between the bars. "Come here! Fast!"

Across the field, near the flagpole, Betty Johnson and her friends were standing in a circle. She was the prettiest girl in class, with long dark hair and dimples, and she always wore deep-colored dresses and black stockings. All the girls who followed her worshipped her. All the others were nothing.

They were over in an instant, crowding around.

Dale and Chad crawled out through the bars to meet them. Freddy followed, but was pushed back inside by Chad, who was bigger and tougher.

"Doesn't Freddy look like Catfish Bob?" Chad exclaimed. "See his sucker mouth!"

Freddy's classmates laughed. Others from around saw something was going on, and thinking it was a fight, ran over to see. They climbed like spiders all over the monkey bars, pale faces poking through and taunting, hissing and pointing. Fredrick stared at his feet, kicked a stone, felt the October coldness creep into his toes. He didn't hear words; he felt their mockery slice from all directions like a bitter wind. He wanted to leave, to climb out, and looked for an escape, but he saw nothing but faces chanting and their breath—wisps of gray vapors like winter venom, spewing. He was trapped.

"Sucker mouth, sucker mouth!" the chant repeated.

But throughout the whole spectacle, through some stroke of luck, he didn't cry.

And then the bell rang and they were gone. *Like ghosts*, Freddy thought.

Red leaves circled in the wind. Dead leaves.

He cried then, with nobody around, then wiped his eyes clear and trotted up the towering steps. He was late for class and had to sit in the corner for an hour and couldn't participate in show-and-tell. But he didn't mind that much. He didn't bring anything to show the class, anyway. Last week he had brought a cap gun to school, and as soon as he had showed it to his classmates, Miss Shepherd had told him that nobody really cared about guns, and that he shouldn't bring it to school anymore. He felt stupid and sat down.

For the next two hours, after he had received permission to return to his seat, pictures circulated around him, some of which he caught a glimpse of, which wasn't an accident. Dale sat in front of him and made sure to hold the pictures up high. They were all of Freddy, his face riddled with whiskers and with a huge sucker mouth and jagged teeth. The caption under each said: "Catfish Freddy."

That was his new name, Catfish Freddy.

So he ignored them and watched his fish. It never moved, just sat there, stuck to the glass or rocks. A few times, Angel darted toward him, but Bob slipped behind a plastic weed, hovering, then sat on the bottom of the tank and didn't move for a long time.

He thought Angel was just being playful. But still, he wasn't sure. So he continued to watch. Then he thought of something. He smiled at first, because he felt smart.

How long did it take for algae to grow in a new tank? Would his fish have enough to eat?

He decided to ask his teacher.

When class was over, Freddy cradled his books and headed toward the door. He waited until Dale and Chad had dressed and left.

"Miss Shepherd?" he said, stopping in front of her desk.

"Have a nice weekend, Freddy."

"My fish—"

She glanced up. "I have work to do, Freddy. Let's talk on Monday, okay?"

Her voice scared him, that quivering and toneless voice she always used with him.

He left without another word.

•••

Catfish Bob was dead by Monday morning.

Freddy stood by the aquarium and stared at the pale body. Half of it was eaten, including the eyes, pecked at by all the other fish, since it was the weekend and the kids weren't there to feed them.

Most of the class thought the act of cannibalism was neat.

Betty, who had her hair in pigtails, pressed her forehead against the glass and her nose wrinkled in disgust, but soon her mouth stretched to a savage smile. She announced, in her quite musical voice, "Maybe we should keep it in there! We can watch the other fish eat its dead body!"

The class went into an uproar.

"Just like piranha!" Dale said, in agreement. "We can feed them dead fish and watch them tear it apart!"

"How about hamburger!" Chad said. "That's what you feed piranha or crocodiles or great white sharks!" He poked at the glass with his huge fingertip, in awe.

More kids voiced their opinions, until Miss Shepherd told everybody to take their seats. She had to drag a dazed Betty Johnson away by her arm and push her down in her seat. Betty continued to stare at the tank, infected by the atrocity.

Miss Shepherd scooped up Catfish Bob in a net and disposed of the remains in the bathroom. When she returned, the class was somewhat back to normal, talking about getting their own aquariums. Some talked about their weekend trick-or-treating and all the candy they got. Others were passing notes and whispering and telling jokes.

Betty still watched the tank, smiling and waiting for more dismemberment. She even smiled at Freddy, once. He smiled back at her. It was then he realized maybe he should hide his interests better, so he wouldn't be the scapegoat in class anymore.

After a few minutes, Miss Shepherd approached Freddy and knelt down beside him. He sat quietly, drawing a picture. When she spoke, her voice sounded softer than normal. "You wanna help me feed Angel from now on?"

Freddy nodded in silence, then went back to his work. He had a sheet of white paper and the pack of crayons on his desk, minus the two colors. He was drawing a picture of all the pretty fish in the aquarium. It was a picture with bright sunshine and beautiful ocean currents. He wanted to draw a picture that would get displayed on the board with all the others.

And later that day, it did.

And if Miss Shepherd would have looked closer, held his picture up to the halogen light like his other drawing, she would have noticed little red spots on all of his fish, all over their colorful little gills.

Aric Sundquist is a writer of speculative fiction. Born and raised in Michigan's Upper Peninsula, he graduated from Northern Michigan University with a Master's degree in Creative Writing. His stories have appeared in numerous publications, including *Fearful Fathoms Vol. 1*, *The Best of Dark Moon Digest*, *Night Terrors III*, *Division by Zero 4: rEvolution*, and *Evil Jester Digest Vol. 1*. He also enjoys tabletop board games, playing guitar, and traveling with his girlfriend. Feel free to visit him at: http://aricsundquist. weebly.com/.

Jon Taylor

A Song Cover

I've been to the U.P.
In the ephemeral month of May
And seen the woods carpeted
To the horizon

In all four directions
With a bloom of spring beauties
Overwhelming the trout lilies
Scattered among them

The scene
Unchanging for miles
As the road wound along
From Munising to Grand Marais

Surely the phenomenon
Has been noted before in song
Even if it has escaped my ears
And I can only write down my own

A Sighting

"I was standing here
Like now at the window
A few weeks ago
And saw a big cat in the side yard

It poked around a few minutes
And then went back in the woods
Without knowing I watched it
The whole time

The dogs had been going crazy
Since a couple days before
Barking their heads off
Whenever we let them outside

I took it for a mountain lion
The tail on the thing looked
About four feet long"
"Well, it wasn't a bobcat then"

Jon Taylor is the author of *Berry Picker's Blues*, a volume of Michigan/Northwoods/Upper Peninsula poems. Jon lives in Nashville, TN, but his spiritual home is "up dere in da woods, eh?"

Sailboats in Mackinac Harbor

The Blueberry Trail

by Tyler Tichelaar

"I see someone finally bought the house across the street from you," said John.

"Yes, but we haven't met him yet," his mother Ellen replied. "I better take the cake out of the oven."

"Grandma, can we eat the cake now?" asked Maddy. She was nearly seven and quite impatient.

"Not yet," said Ellen, opening the oven and pulling out the cake with hot pads. "It has to cool. We'll go blueberry picking, and when we get home, we'll have supper and then the cake."

"That's a long time from now," said Maddy.

"You won't starve before then," John told her.

"Why do we have to go pick blueberries?" asked Neil, age ten, lifting his head from his Harry Potter book for the first time since they'd arrived at Grandpa and Grandma's house. John, who was an author, wished he could find readers as interested in the books he wrote.

"Because then we can have blueberry pie," Ellen replied. "John, holler to your father that we're leaving now."

John opened the patio screen door and called to Tom, who was out in his garden.

"Dad, we're going blueberry picking now. We'll be back about five, in time for supper."

"Okay!" Tom hollered back.

"Here are the pails," said Grandma, collecting them from the closet and passing them out to everyone.

In another minute, they were walking down the driveway. They crossed the street and started up the trail into the empty wooded lot next to the neighbor's house. Just as they started up the trail, a car pulled into the neighbor's yard.

"That must be your new neighbor," said John.

"Must be," said Ellen, but she could not stop to meet him now. She was too busy trying not to be pulled over by Maddy, who was holding her hand and trying to skip down the trail. Seventy-one-year-old grandmothers rarely skip.

Every first week of August or so, John would bring the kids to his parents' house to go blueberry picking. Usually his wife Wendy would also come, but she had a meeting in town that evening. Ellen decided that gave her an excuse to feed John and her grandkids. As for John, he loved to go blueberry picking, although he didn't remember the squatting down hurting quite as much when he was a kid. Now that he had passed forty, he wondered how many more blueberry-picking years he had left, but there was his mother at seventy-one having no qualms about going berry picking.

They had a few accidents that afternoon. Maddy got into an ant nest and had to be brushed off; fortunately, she was brave enough not to scream—at least not much. Neil spilled all the berries out of his bucket, but not quite accidentally. He had discovered that if he swung his basket upside down in a circle fast enough, he could do so without losing any blueberries. Unfortunately, about the ninetieth time, he didn't swing it quite fast enough and the berries fell onto the dirt trail.

"It's all right," Ellen told Neil as he and John retrieved them. "We'll just rinse them off, and anyway, my mother always used to say, 'You have to eat a peck of dirt before you die.'"

"What's a peck?" asked Maddy.

"I guess I don't really know," said Ellen. "Just a lot of dirt, I guess."

"That's gross!" said Maddy.

Soon it was five o'clock and they were heading back down the trail toward home. As they approached the neighbor's house, they could see him in his backyard.

He saw them, too, and he started walking through the woods toward them.

"Your new neighbor is heading this way," John told Ellen.

"Oh," said Ellen as John waved at him.

The neighbor did not wave back. He walked a few steps closer and then said, "This is private property."

"What's private property?" Maddy asked Grandma.

"Shh," Ellen hushed.

"We're your neighbors," said John. "At least, my mother is, but I grew up here."

"It's nice to meet you," said Ellen. "I'm Ellen and my husband is Tom. This is my son, John, and my grandchildren, Neil and Maddy."

"I'm sorry if we're intruding," John said when the man did not reply.

"I own this property."

"Yes," said John. "We know, but this trail has been here since before the neighborhood started forty years ago. It's an old snowmobile trail and people walk down it all the time. It's a popular walking trail."

"Maybe so," said the man, "but not anymore. Now I'd appreciate it if you'd respect the law and not trespass on it any longer."

"Well," said Ellen, under her breath.

"Where are you from?" asked John.

"Grosse Pointe," said the man, "not that that matters."

"What brings you up to the U.P.?" John asked.

"I'm a doctor at the hospital."

"My mom worked at the hospital," said John. "She was the longest employee there when she retired a few years ago."

"I was there forty-two years," added Ellen, as if that would help the situation.

The man did not reply, unless flaring his nostrils counted.

"Well, it was nice meeting you," said Ellen, who had been raised to be polite. Then she and her family turned to walk home.

"The nerve of that man," said Ellen once they were out of his hearing.

"Yeah, the nerve of him!" said Neil. "It's our Blueberry Trail!"

"Shh, Neil," said John. "Don't be rude, and it's not our trail. It is his property."

"It doesn't surprise me he's from downstate," said Ellen. "Those people are always coming up here trying to change things. Humph!"

In a few more minutes, they were inside the house and it was time for supper. Tom was called inside to eat, and soon the neighbor was forgotten.

•••

"Do you remember the new neighbor?" asked Ellen a couple of days later when she and John were talking on the phone.

"How could I forget?" John replied.

"Well, guess what he did," said Ellen.

"Sell his house and move back downstate?" John asked hopefully.

"No," said Ellen. "He put up a big No Trespassing sign. Planted it on a stick right in the middle of the trail."

"You're kidding," said John.

"No. It makes me so mad. It's one thing if he doesn't want people walking on his trail, but he doesn't need to put up an eyesore like that, and it's not a small sign either. It must be a couple of feet wide—black with ugly orange letters. It even says, 'Violators will be prosecuted.' Can you believe that?"

"What kind of an idiot tries to make enemies with all of his neighbors the minute he moves in?" asked John.

"An idiot from downstate apparently," said Ellen.

•••

John fumed about the No Trespassing sign all that evening. By bedtime, Wendy was sick of hearing about it.

"John," she said, "like it or not, it is his property, so he can do whatever he wants on it."

"I know it," said John, crawling into bed next to her, "but it's not a matter of what's legal. It's the principle of the thing. How is it hurting him if people walk down that trail? Nobody is damaging his property."

"Even so, it is his property," said Wendy.

•••

The next day, John called his mother.

"I'm so mad about that No Trespassing sign," he said.

"So am I," said Ellen, "but what can we do?"

"I don't know," said John. "I was thinking maybe I could go over and talk to him, but I don't think he'll listen."

"No, I don't think he will. Your father was outside this morning mowing the lawn and waved to him, but the guy didn't wave back."

"Who acts that way toward his neighbors?" asked John.

Ellen didn't answer, but after a second, she said, "Oh, it doesn't matter. Your dad and I can drive out onto the Sands Plains to go blueberry picking, and besides, in a few more years we'll probably want to sell this house and move in to Marquette."

John didn't want to think about that. How could they ever sell the house, especially with Dickens buried in the backyard? After nearly twenty years, John still mourned his canine friend.

"I wish we could do something," said John. "Maybe we could write a petition for all the neighbors to sign, saying they want him to keep the Blueberry Trail open and promising they won't damage his property."

"I don't think you'll get many people to sign that," said Ellen. "I hardly even know any of the neighbors up the street anymore. Everyone moved away after their kids grew up."

"Jane would sign it," said John.

"Oh, I don't know. Jane isn't doing all that well. I doubt she'll last through the winter."

"But she could still sign a petition," said John.

"She'll never walk down that trail again," said Ellen.

"But surely she'd want everyone else to know the joy of walking down the Blueberry Trail."

"Maybe. You could ask her," said Ellen, "but one signature isn't going to make much difference."

"No, but you and Dad could sign it."

"Not if no one else does," said Ellen. "I don't want the neighbor any madder at me than he already is."

"Mr. Richmond would sign it," said John.

"Yes, but what difference will that make since he lives in Texas now?"

"What about the Hautamakis?" John persisted.

"They moved into Lost Creek last winter," said Ellen. "I'm trying to talk your dad into us moving there."

John could see this conversation wasn't helping matters.

•••

That evening while they were making supper, John asked Wendy, "What if I offered to buy the property the Blueberry Trail is on?"

"John," she said, sighing.

"Well, I mean, I could buy it and put up a big sign that says, 'The Blueberry Trail Is Open' or 'Welcome to the Blueberry Trail. Free Public Access.'"

"John," Wendy repeated.

"Well, I just hate to see it not used. It was a big part of my childhood. In the summer, I'd walk Dickens down that trail almost every day, and Chad and I used to ride our bikes down it—sometimes all the way to Harvey. It just...it means a lot to me."

"I know," said Wendy, putting her hand on his shoulder. "But life changes."

"I know," said John, "but it sucks."

"Mommy, Daddy said, 'Sucks,'" said Maddy, who happened to enter the kitchen at that moment.

"I heard him," said Wendy, "but that doesn't give you an excuse to say it. Now go wash your hands before we eat."

WHERE RAIL AND WATER MEET AT ST. IGNACE, MICH.

St Ignace waterfront railroad

"Doesn't Daddy get grounded or not get his dessert or something?" Maddy demanded.

"I'll punish him while you wash up," said Wendy.

"I want to watch," said Maddy.

"Go!" John ordered. Maddy knew from John's tone that she had better do what he said.

"John," said Wendy, once Maddy was gone, "you don't need to snap at her. I think you're blowing this whole Blueberry Trail thing way out of proportion."

To keep from snapping at Wendy, John decided he better go wash his hands, too.

•••

The next day, John went to visit Aunt Eleanor. Actually, she was his great-aunt, and less than two months from turning one hundred. Everyone was hoping she'd live to see the big birthday bash the family was planning, and so far, it looked like she would.

Aunt Eleanor's daughter Lucy was there with her when John arrived. Her sister Maud had gone out grocery shopping. Both daughters were in their seventies and retired. John asked Aunt Eleanor how she was feeling since she'd been in the hospital for a couple of days earlier that week after complaining she was tired, the result of her congestive heart failure. But she was a stubborn old woman, not one to admit she had anything wrong with her except to her daughters, and when she did that, you knew she really didn't feel well.

"I'm fine. My girls are taking good care of me," said Aunt Eleanor.

"I know they are," said John, smiling at Lucy. "I'm sure they're glad to have you back home."

"For a while there," said Aunt Eleanor, "I didn't think the doctor would let me come home, but I got my wish."

"Your mother says you've been out picking blueberries," Lucy said to John. "Did you get many?"

"Oh, yes," said John. "Almost a pail-full, though Neil spilled most of his."

"I wish I could go blueberry picking," said Aunt Eleanor, "but I know that's a wish I won't see fulfilled."

"Oh, well," said John. "Blueberry picking is a lot of hard work, so I wouldn't mind missing it so much if I were you, not so long as you can still enjoy blueberry pie."

"I can definitely do that," said Aunt Eleanor, laughing, "and also blueberry soup."

John grimaced. Aunt Eleanor knew he hated blueberry soup. She had made it for him once when he was a teenager and he had been rude enough to tell her it tasted like paint. Since then, she had never quit kidding him about it.

"You can keep your blueberry soup," he said, smirking.

"I had many years of blueberry picking, though," said Aunt Eleanor. "I remember when I was a little girl and we used to take the blueberry train up toward Big Bay to pick them. We'd go for the whole day and have so much fun up there."

"Who went?" John asked.

"Oh, all of us usually. My ma and pa, and your grandpa and Roy and Bill and Ada," she said, listing off her siblings. John's grandpa had been her oldest brother.

"I wish I could have gone with you back then," said John. "I'd have loved to have seen all of you when you were kids."

"Sometimes," said Aunt Eleanor, "when I close my eyes, I feel like I'm still there, in the middle of a pine tree copse, surrounded by blueberry bushes and my brothers and sisters all hollering to each other, and...."

And then Aunt Eleanor teared up a little.

"Do you want a Kleenex, Mom?" asked Lucy.

"No, I'm okay. I just miss them is all, but I'm with them again when I close my eyes like that. I was lucky to grow up in a good family like I did."

"So am I," said John.

"I know you know about these things, John," said Aunt Eleanor. "That's why you're a writer. You just hang onto those memories because they'll always be there to comfort you, even when the blueberries are long gone and all the people you loved have passed on. They'll always be there in your memory."

"Yes," said John. "I know."

But he realized he had needed to be reminded of it.

•••

When John got home that afternoon, the house was quiet. Wendy and the kids had gone back-to-school shopping. If he was lucky, he might be able to spend a little time working on his novel.

John made his way into his study and sat down at his desk. He booted up his computer and found the place where he had left off writing. He started to read over the last few paragraphs, but as he read, he found his thoughts going back to what Aunt Eleanor had said, and then he found himself closing his eyes.

After a moment, he could see Dickens in front of him, his tail wagging, and he could feel the sandy path beneath his tennis shoes, and yes, when he turned to look, he could see blueberries there, ripening along the trailside.

Tyler R. Tichelaar is the author of *My Marquette, The Best Place, The Gothic Wanderer, Haunted Marquette*, and numerous other books. When not writing his own books, he is busy editing those of other authors. Find out more about Tyler and his books at www.MarquetteFiction.com.

Cedena's Surprise

by Donna Winters

Fayette, Upper Michigan
Monday, May 8, 1893

"What's troubling you, child?" Aunt Catherine hobbled on a wobbly cane to the parlor window where Cedena held back the worn lace curtain and stared out at Snail Shell Harbor.

Father's old Mackinaw boat bobbed on the cerulean swells that pushed it through the port entrance toward its mooring on the eight-hundred-foot dock. Cedena could make out Father's sturdy profile at the stern and that of Uncle Eugene stooped near the centerboard. She prayed they'd caught plenty of fish today. Times had been tough since the iron-smelting furnace had shut down two-and-a-half years ago. Cedena had been twenty then, and hoping to marry, but the best prospects for a husband had moved away.

Yet that wasn't what gnawed at Cedena. Mother and Father's twenty-fifth anniversary was coming up on the last day of June and what Cedena wanted more than anything else was to buy them a nice gift and put on a surprise party, one that would include the entire community. After all, there was hardly a soul in town who hadn't been helped by Mother or Father at some time. Surely their friends and neighbors would want to honor their special day. But with only a few dollars to call her own, how could Cedena purchase a gift and put on a party, let alone keep the gathering a surprise in this tight-knit community?

Cedena turned to Aunt Catherine, whose bent frame was nearly a foot shorter than her own five-foot two-inch height. "I'll tell you what's troubling me. I'd like to celebrate Mother and Father's silver anniversary with a gift and a surprise party, but how, with no money?"

The back door thudded. Mother was evidently home from her trip to the General Store and Post Office. Her voice preceded her into the parlor.

"There's a letter from my sister, and the return address is *not* Kansas City. Guess where Nancy is now."

Aunt Catherine gave Cedena a quick hug. "We'll discuss your problem later."

Cedena nodded and turned from the window to face Mother. "Is Aunt Nancy in Chicago?"

Mother drew a sharp breath. "How did you know?"

"Didn't she say in her last letter that she wanted to see the World's Columbian Exposition when it opened up? I've envied her ever since. The stories about the Fair in the newspaper are simply fascinating."

Mother sat on the love seat, reached for the letter opener on the marble-top side table, and slid it beneath the flap. "It must have been five months ago, in her Christmas letter, that Nancy wrote about the Fair, and even *I* did not recall that she was going there until I saw the postmark on her letter."

Cedena joined Mother on the love seat as she eased the gilt-edged sheet of ecru vellum from its wrapper. She stared at the precise, tiny cursive, held it as far from her as her arms could reach, and then passed it to Cedena with a sigh.

Wilson passenger service between Pickford and the Soo

"You read it. My glasses are in the other room, and I'm not sure that even *they* would be strong enough to bring that tiny script into focus."

Cedena smoothed out the folds. "Aunt Nancy sure packs a lot onto a page. The letter is dated the second of May. 'My dear Isabella, Charles, Cedena, Aunt Catherine, and Uncle Eugene, You simply *must'*— must is underlined—'come to the Fair. James and I attended the Grand Opening yesterday and the word "Grand" can hardly do it justice. To start things off, a six hundred piece band played a march specially composed for the occasion. We couldn't see the band for the tens of thousands of folks standing in front of us, but the paper says it was six hundred and we have no reason to doubt it. Then a prayer was offered by the Senate Chaplain.

Soon after, President Cleveland pressed the gold button to start the machinery in motion. Fountains sprang up and lights sparkled, the wonders of electricity putting on such an amazing show I doubt anyone watching will ever forget it. At least *we* will not.

"'In the afternoon, James went to attend his company's display in the Manufactures Building while I went to the opening of the Woman's Building. Mrs. Potter Palmer gave a fine speech followed by more speechifying by the Countess of Aberdeen. The building and all its contents were designed by women. It was simply amazing. Every American female should see it for herself.

"'And every American male owes it to himself to visit the Manufacturers Building. Charles would love all forty acres of it. Yes, forty acres under one roof, enough room to easily get lost. Charles must also take in the Fisheries Building, Machinery Hall, the Transportation Building, the Spanish Caravel, and the Viking ship.

"'So come. James and I will gladly forward the cost of your boat or train tickets, and will pay your entrance fees, room, and board, once you're here. We look forward to hearing from you with the particulars of your travel plans. We will remain in Chicago until the closing of the Fair at the end of October. Best to come in summer, though, so please don't delay!

"'With all our love, James and Nancy.'"

Cedena lifted her gaze. Mother's head was already moving from side to side.

"Mother, if money is no issue, why can't we go?"

"Your father would never approve. He has too much pride to allow my sister to pay our way."

Aunt Catherine thumped her cane on the pine floor. "You should at least ask Charles."

Mother's mouth drew into a condemning smile. "Are we to leave you and Uncle Eugene here to fend for yourselves while we go cavorting off to the Fair? The cooking, cleaning up, washing, and ironing, would tax your feeble bodies into the grave. We will in no way be a party to such fatal circumstances."

Aunt Catherine threw her head back and chortled so loud, Cedena was sure she heard it echo off the limestone bluff on the other side of the harbor.

Mother stared grim-faced at Aunt Catherine, who pulled her handkerchief from her sleeve and dabbed tears from her cheeks before making a reply.

"Isabella, you think much too highly of yourself. Eugene and I are not nearly as helpless as you say."

Mother turned to Cedena. "I will compose a letter right now declining Nancy's offer. Would you please take it to the Post Office? I'll have it ready in just a few minutes."

"Certainly, Mother. I think I'll write a note to include with it." Cedena climbed the stairs to her loft room and sat down at her slant top desk. Hastily, she composed a cordial note to her aunt with banal news of weather and health. Then she took out a second sheet of stationery and quickly wrote another missive, blotted the ink, folded it, and tucked it into her skirt pocket.

With her first letter in hand, Cedena descended the stairs to the parlor where Mother was just finishing her own correspondence at the secretary. Cedena handed her letter to Mother who gave it a cursory read, then folded it with her own and tucked them into the envelope.

"I'll seal it for you, Mother."

"Would you, dear? I must fire up the stove and get cooking if we're to have dinner on time."

Mother headed into the kitchen and Cedena sat down at the secretary. Making sure that Mother was truly out of sight, Cedena slipped the letter out of her pocket and into the envelope. Aunt Catherine cleared her throat. Cedena glanced up and tapped her finger to her lips.

Aunt Catherine grinned and wiggled her brows.

When Cedena had sealed the envelope, she went to Aunt Catherine and whispered in her ear.

"I've told Aunt Nancy and Uncle James I'm planning a surprise party for Mother and Father on the thirtieth of June and invited them to come. They're to make their reply to Mrs. Johnson so Mother won't know. Now, you'll have to help me plan the celebration."

Aunt Catherine nodded and whispered back. "We will do it up right. Now be off with you to the Post Office. And stop by Johnsons' on your way home and let them know. I'm sure they'll help us plan the party."

Cedena snatched her shawl from the peg beside the door and stepped out into the late afternoon sun. The fresh lake breeze ruffled the shawl fringe and flapped at her black cotton skirt as she marched down the crushed limestone and slag path toward the General Store where the Post Office was located. Then her troubling thought returned. How could she plan a party and buy a gift if she had no money?

Inside the store, Cedena paused in front of the outgoing mail slot, said a little prayer that Aunt Nancy and Uncle James would come, and sent the invitation on its way.

"Letter to a beau?" Mr. Bennet, the proprietor and Postmaster, stepped from behind the wall of mail boxes.

"No, it's to my Aunt Nancy."

"That was fast. Your mother just picked up a letter from her sister not more than an hour ago. But the return address was Chicago, not Kansas City. And the postmark was the World's Columbian Exposition."

No surprise that Mr. Bennet, with his sharp eye for news and his glib tongue for spreading speculation, had taken notice. "Aunt Nancy and Uncle James are at the Fair on business until it closes."

Mr. Bennet nodded. "Lucky for them. I've a mind to take my wife and make a trip down there to see what all the fuss is about."

"Who would watch the store and sort the mail?"

"Precisely the problem when you're married to your assistant. Unless I solve it, I guess we'll both stay right here."

Cedena turned to go.

"Wait up, young lady."

Cedena paused, her hand on the door knob.

"You wouldn't be willing to learn how things are run here so Mrs. Bennet and I can get to the Fair, would you? There's a dollar a day in it for you while we're away. No pay while you train, though."

Cedena returned to the postal counter. "When did you plan to go?"

"Soon as you learn the routine. When can you begin training?"

"Tomorrow?"

"Be here at eight o'clock and plan to stay the day."

"Yes, sir! See you then."

Cedena was so excited about the prospect of earning her own money that she hurried right past the Johnsons' house and had to turn around halfway up Stewart Street and retrace her steps. She gave her special knock on the back door—three rapid taps, a pause, and two taps. Sarah opened the door.

"You'll never guess what just happened!" Cedena's smile stretched so tightly she was sure she'd split her lips.

"Do tell."

"Mr. Bennet hired me to tend the store and Post Office while he and Mrs. Bennet go to the Fair!"

"That's wonderful! What do you plan to do with all that money? Splurge on some new

trifles from that big catalog Mr. Bennet keeps on his counter?"

Cedena shook her head. "I need to talk to you and your mother about an idea I have."

Sarah turned toward the kitchen and gestured for Cedena to follow.

The tempting aroma of chicken stew rose from the pot Mrs. Johnson was stirring. Cedena greeted her and explained about the anniversary party, Uncle James and Aunt Nancy, and her new job at the General Store that would make a gift and surprise party possible.

Mrs. Johnson set her wooden spoon aside and turned to Cedena with a smile. "Those sound like wonderful plans! I hope you won't be working on June 30th."

"I don't think so. I start training tomorrow, and as soon as I learn how things work, Mr. and Mrs. Bennet will go to the Fair. Seems to me they should be back before the end of next month. Now that I know I'll have money for a party and a gift, I'll need your help organizing and deciding on something nice."

Sarah grinned. "You could give your folks a beautiful tea service engraved in honor of the occasion."

Mrs. Johnson shook her head. "I'm not sure your mother would have much opportunity to use it. You'd better think on it awhile. Perhaps ask your Aunt Catherine for ideas. There's time yet."

Cedena backed toward the door. "You're right. I'd better get home. Mother will wonder why I'm not there to help her get dinner on."

•••

At home, as Cedena prepared to set the table, she told Mother about working for the Bennets.

"Nice, dear. Now would you please mash the potatoes as soon as you finish setting the table? We need to get supper on before this poached salmon turns to rubber."

When the family had gathered at the table, the blessing had been said, and the fish, mashed potatoes, and spring peas had been served, Cedena focused on Father. "We received a most delightful letter from Aunt Nancy today. She told all about the opening day of the Fair. You'll have to read it after dinner. It was quite something. She wants us all to come to the Fair, and even offered to pay our expenses!"

"Is that so?" Father mumbled the words in between bites.

"Yes, but Mother has already written back and said we aren't coming."

Father's fork, laden with another mouthful of mashed potatoes, paused mid-air and then made a slow descent to his plate as his gaze shifted to Mother. "You turned Nancy down without even telling me?"

Mother drew a quick breath and put on her mollifying smile. "Of course, Charles. Since the day we married, you've made it clear that you hate to be beholden to anyone. And it's a simple fact that we haven't the means to pay for such a trip."

Father's eyes darkened as the forkful of mashed potatoes ascended again and disappeared into his mouth.

Uncle Eugene's silver mustache quirked as he grinned at Father. "It's all settled, simple as that, Charles. While you and I sail out and cast our nets, decisions are made for us—I mean *you*—by your very competent and efficient mate. Must say I envy Nancy and James. If I were two decades younger, I'd go down to Chicago, no question about it. I'd like to read that letter of Nancy's when you're done with it."

Mother sighed. "Enough about that. Cedena, tell your father and Uncle Eugene what you'll be doing tomorrow for the Bennets."

•••

On the following Saturday, when her first week of training was over, Cedena grabbed a new copy of the weekly Escanaba newspaper and headed for home. As she made her way up Stewart Avenue in dancing shadows of hardwoods that had yet to unfurl their leaves, she mused about her work at the General Store. Yes, she had learned how to wait on customers in the store and Post Office, but mostly she had helped to clean and rearrange the store and inventory. It was as if Mr. and Mrs. Bennet wanted cleaning help but didn't want to pay for it. And since the

work was only half done, they had asked her to come back on Monday for another week. Oh, well, it would be worth it when Mr. Bennet paid her for tending the store while they visited the Fair.

How she envied them. If only Mother and Father would swallow their pride and change their minds about going. But that was as likely as a snowstorm in June.

Cedena opened the newspaper to skim the front page. A headline and subtitles halted her steps. "Charges at Chicago. Cost of Rooms at Hotels and Private Houses. Visitors to the World's Fair may make the cost of their stay large or small as they choose. How to do it." A long article followed. She couldn't take time to read it now, but after Father and Uncle Eugene had finished with the paper, she would read every word. If she couldn't go to the Fair in person, at least she would learn how others would do it.

•••

Later that night, after the others had gone to bed, Cedena sat alone in the parlor and read about the Fair by the light of an oil lamp. Not only did she learn how to visit Chicago, but also in a separate article on page seven, she read about the highlights of the Fair, the best buildings to visit in a short amount of time. When she finished, she folded the paper, carried it to the kitchen, and tossed it onto the stack of kindling in the wood box beside the stove. Tomorrow, it would go up in flames, just as her hopes for ever visiting the Fair had done. Why did she antagonize herself so by reading those articles? With a heavy heart she climbed the stairs, undressed, and crawled into bed. Sleep came amidst a load of resentment that Aunt Nancy's offer had been dismissed so efficiently.

•••

A week later, on Cedena's way home from her last day of training at the General Store, she fought to hold back her tears. She mustn't let Mother see how upset she was. Taking a deep breath, she stepped inside and headed for the sitting room.

Aunt Catherine sat in her rocker working her knitting needles. She glanced up briefly. "Cedena, you're home. Your mother is at the Johnsons. Won't be back for a while."

Cedena let her tears flow. "Oh, Aunt Catherine...the worst possible thing has happened." She sobbed into her handkerchief.

"Now, now, child. Come and tell old Aunt Catherine what's troubling you. It can't be as bad as all that, eh?" She moved to the sofa and motioned for Cedena to join her.

Cedena dabbed away her tears. "The Bennets—they're not going to the Fair until July. I won't have any money for a party or a gift for Mother and Father's anniversary. And to think I've already invited Aunt Nancy and Uncle James!" Cedena blew her nose.

"You will *too* be able to give them a party and a gift. The party needn't cost money. Folks will bring food to share. As for a gift, come with me."

Aunt Catherine headed for the room off the parlor that she shared with Uncle Eugene. She stooped to raise the lid on the battered, hide-covered trunk at the foot of their four-poster bed. Neatly folded woolen sweaters lay on top and the scent of herbal moth repellant sachets wafted up—lavender, rosemary, clove, and cedar. The aroma calmed Cedena.

Aunt Catherine pulled the sweaters back and reached down deep into the corner, coming up with something the size of a can wrapped in muslin. She sat on the bed and patted the space next to her.

Cedena sat down as Aunt Catherine peeled back the muslin one layer at a time. A badly tarnished silver cup with vine engravings and a winged handle emerged. "This is a coin cup. Eugene and I celebrated our twenty-fifth anniversary in 1862, long before we moved here from New York State with your folks. Our friends and neighbors took up a collection of silver coins and had them made into this cup. We could give it to your folks for *their* anniversary. We'd have to change the inscription on the bottom is all."

Cedena took the cup and read the inscription. "'To Catherine and Eugene on their 25th anniversary.' Why would you want to give this away? It was made especially for you, and it's so beautiful." She fingered the vine engravings.

Aunt Catherine shrugged. "I kept it on display until we moved to Fayette in '68. With living quarters tight, I couldn't seem to find a place for it. If you could give this a good polishing and have the inscription reworded, we could present it to your folks. It would do my heart good to hand it down to someone in the family. I'll bet Mr. Bennet knows an engraver who can do the work. It shouldn't cost much. I'll give you the money. Do you think you could polish it up when your mother isn't around and take it to Mr. Bennet?"

"Sure."

The back door thudded. "Cedena? Aunt Catherine?"

Cedena shoved the cup into Aunt Catherine's hands and hurried out of the room to intercept her mother.

•••

On the evening of June 30th, Cedena, dressed in her Sunday best, gazed about the hotel dining room. Thank goodness the hotel manager had owed Mrs. Johnson a favor and she had been able to reserve the space at no charge.

Everything was in order. Paper streamers had been strung from silver bells at the center of the ceiling to all corners of the room. A banner hung behind the head table with silver lettering. "Happy 25th Anniversary Isabella and Charles." Aunt Nancy and Uncle James were already seated at the head table with Uncle Eugene and Aunt Catherine. The Bennets and Johnsons as well as many of the fishing families had already filled the other tables. Along the side wall, a table laden with food provided by each family waited in readiness for the meal to begin. And on a small table in the far corner stood the beautifully decorated five-layer white and chocolate cake that would bring the meal to a sweet and satisfying conclusion. The coin cup, reinscribed, had been wrapped by Aunt Nancy in silk and tied with a lovely silver bow. Cedena would present it at the very end.

Cedena checked the clock. It wouldn't be long now. Father had promised Mother an anniversary dinner at the hotel with reservations at six, neither of them suspecting that a party lay in wait. Little Johnny LaFarge was keeping watch on Stewart Avenue and would let everyone know when the guests of honor were approaching.

None of this would have been possible without Mrs. Johnson and Sarah. They had helped to notify neighbors, decorate the room, bake the cake, and coordinate the menu. Odd, though, how often Cedena had run into Sarah at the General Store in the past couple of weeks. It was almost as if she were helping out there. But that couldn't be. In two days, the Bennets would be away and Cedena would be in charge of the store and Post Office.

Johnny ran into the dining room and shouted. "They're coming! They're coming!"

Cedena made her way to the dining room entrance while Johnny took a seat with his folks, and a hush fell over the entire room. Cedena's heart pounded. Had Mother or Father suspected? Would this truly be the surprise she had planned?

Lord, let this be a night to remember.

The hotel door opened. Cedena peeked past the dining room entrance. Mother looked lovely in her navy blue silk dress with the white lace collar and white silk rose at the waistline. She had pulled her hair into a twist held by the tortoise shell comb Father had given her some years ago. And he was looking dapper in his gray coat and waistcoat, charcoal gray pants, short turnover shirt collar, and floppy bowtie. Cedena pulled back as their footsteps neared. When they reached the open doorway, she signaled the guests for their unison greeting.

"Surprise! Happy 25th Anniversary!"

Mother staggered back, her face pale. Father wrapped his arm about her. Cedena flanked Mother on the other side and with Father's help, ushered her into the room.

"Happy Anniversary, Mother, Father! As you can see, the whole town as well as Aunt Nancy and Uncle James have come to celebrate your special occasion. Let's get you seated at the head table and I'll bring you something to eat."

Mother surveyed the room. "I can't believe it! And here I thought it would just be the two of us!"

As Cedena led Mother and Father to the head table, they thanked their neighbors and friends for coming, and marveled that the party had been kept a complete secret.

At the head table, Aunt Nancy, stunning in her burgundy dress with wide sleeves that narrowed at the elbow, stood and pulled Mother into a hug. "Congratulations, Isabella!" She glanced up at Father. "You, too, Charles! I'm so glad Cedena told us about your party. Do sit down. I'll help Cedena bring your dinners."

With Aunt Nancy's help, Cedena soon had Mother, Father, Aunt Catherine, and Uncle Eugene served from the dishes of salmon, trout, perch, chicken, boiled potatoes, baked beans, string beans, canned peaches, freshly baked dinner rolls, and pasties. For beverages, there were pitchers of water, lemonade, and milk, and pots of coffee. When Cedena and Aunt Nancy had filled plates for themselves and Uncle James, Mrs. Johnson directed the remaining guests to serve themselves, starting with the table nearest the door.

Conversation with Aunt Nancy and Uncle James was filled with fascinating descriptions of the Fair, from the Hawaiian volcano that erupted at regular intervals to the 'fakirs' that swindled folks on the Midway.

"But the best part of the Fair, by far, is the Ferris Wheel." Uncle James sunk his fork into a sizeable piece of chicken. "Nancy and I got a ride on it the day before we left. It's a sight to behold, and the view of the fairgrounds and Lake Michigan...." He let out a low whistle and then jammed the chicken into his mouth.

Cedena tamped down resentment over Mother's ironclad decision not to attend the Fair. Why was she being so unfair when there was nothing to be lost by going? Cedena pushed those thoughts aside to take in more of Aunt Nancy and Uncle James's descriptions.

Too soon, it seemed, the meal was at an end and it was time for cake. Mrs. Johnson and Sarah served. When each guest had received a piece, Cedena fetched the gift, brought it to her folks, and tapped her spoon against her cup to catch everyone's attention.

"I'd like to present Mother and Father with their anniversary gift from Aunt Catherine, Uncle Eugene, and me." She placed the keepsake in Mother's hands.

Mother carefully untied the bow and pulled back the silk fabric. The silver coin cup gleamed.

Mother drew a sharp breath and held the cup high for everyone to see. "Isn't this stunning? Thank you, Cedena, Aunt Catherine, and Uncle Eugene."

"Turn it over, Mother, and read the inscription."

Mother turned the cup upside down. "'To Isabella and Charles on your 25th Anniversary.'"

Mr. Bennet stood and raised his water glass. "Hear, hear! To Isabella and Charles!"

The toast echoed throughout the room and glasses clinked.

Aunt Nancy rested her hand on Mother's arm. "Isabella, don't you have an announcement to make?"

Mother nodded and then clapped her hands until silence reigned again. "Thank you, everyone, for coming to this wonderful party! It certainly was a big surprise. Now, I have an even bigger one. For my daughter, anyway." She set her gaze on Cedena. "Tomorrow, you, your Father, and I are going to the Fair. Nancy, James, and the Bennets will be traveling with us."

Thoughts scattered in Cedena's mind like confetti. Certainly she couldn't have heard right. "What did you say?"

Mother grinned. "I said we're going to the Fair. *You're* going to the Fair. Tomorrow!"

"But...I'm supposed to be working at the store on Monday while the Bennets go."

Mother shook her head. "Sarah will do it. She's been training for a while now."

Mr. Bennet approached. "Cedena, that day I told you Mrs. Bennet and I had postponed our trip—that was because your mother and father had come to us and said they wanted to join us and bring you, too, but it was to be a surprise for you. I couldn't let them leave town before this party you had planned, so I put them off until July. Then I asked Sarah to come and train."

So that was why Cedena had seen Sarah in the store so often in recent days.

Mr. Bennet took Cedena's hand in his and deposited several silver dollars into her palm. "That's for the two weeks you worked for me and Mrs. Bennet. I'm going to enjoy watching you spend every last cent of it at the Fair."

Cedena rose on tiptoe and kissed Mr. Bennet on the cheek. "Thank you!"

He gave a nod and returned to his seat.

A short while later, as Cedena walked home with her family, it was as if she were walking on air. This night of surprises had certainly surpassed her expectations. She turned to Mother.

"What made you change your mind about going to the Fair?"

Father laughed. "You mean *who*. I gave her a tongue lashing after I found out she'd turned down Nancy and James's offer."

"A scolding I no doubt deserved. And Aunt Catherine had some words to say about it, too. Then I read some of those articles in the paper about the Fair and decided to eat my words. I wrote to Nancy and told her I'd changed my mind but I wanted to keep the trip a last minute surprise for you, so she wrote to me in care of Martha so you wouldn't know. Martha offered to check in on Aunt Catherine and Uncle Eugene while we're away, so I had no reason not to go."

Cedena wrapped her arm about Mother's waist and gave it a squeeze. "Thank you, Mother. I thought I was giving you and Father a surprise tonight, but the big surprise turned out to be the one you gave me!"

Donna Winters is the author of more than twenty books including the *Great Lakes Romances® Series,* and *Adventures with Vinnie,* a memoir of the most unpredictable shelter dog ever to join the Winters family. Donna lived her first sixty-five years in states bordering on the Great Lakes. Twelve of those years were spent in the Upper Peninsula. *In 2015, Donna and her husband moved to New Mexico. She is now developing stories set in the southwest. You can find her books on Amazon and at her website, BigwaterPublishing. com.*

The Final Catch

by Jan ("Jon") Wisniewski

"Going fishing?" twenty-year-old Jonny asked his thirty-two-year-old brother Rich as Rich collected his rod and tackle box from the front porch.

"Yup. I've been promising myself for weeks that I'm going to Wolf Point to fish for some brown trout and now I'm finally going!" Rich proclaimed as he angled the rod through the front door.

"Oh!" Rich said as he pushed the door back open with his shoulder before it closed. "Can you grab my blue shirt lying on the chair right there and bring it out here?"

Johnny picked up the shirt and followed Rich out the door. "Thanks," Rich said as he took the shirt from Jonny after he placed the rod and tackle box in the back of his truck.

"Wish I was going with you, but I gotta go to work in a few hours," Jonny said as Rich was putting the shirt on.

"Well, I'll just make you jealous when I come back with a few big ones," Rich said as he took out the snuff can that made a ring in his shirt pocket.

Putting a pinch of snuff in his bottom lip, Rich said, "And I'll be thinking of you and laughing when I reel in my first big one!"

"Thanks. That makes me feel really special!" Jonny smirked, knowing that his brother liked to give him a hard time.

"I'll be on the lake in about an hour. See ya later, Buckshot," Rich said as he started the truck and began to drive off to Misery Bay where he would begin his voyage to Wolf Point.

"If you catch any, I expect fish for dinner tomorrow!" Jonny yelled as Rich was pulling out of the driveway. Rich just chuckled and waved goodbye.

As Jonny watched the red Dodge truck with the nineteen-foot canoe sticking out of the box turn right onto the highway, little did he know that those would be the last words he would ever say to his brother.

Rich began humming to himself while on the highway. Several memories ran through Rich's mind of the times he fished around Wolf Point. Many brown trout, lake trout, rainbow trout, and whitefish were claimed in those waters, and Rich knew where they hid by visually aligning his canoe with the trees and rocks he used as markers on the shoreline. He loved being there by himself, knowing that very few people ventured the more than five miles across Misery Bay to enjoy the bounty of fish residing in those waters.

Thoughts of the many close calls also surfaced where Lake Superior almost didn't allow him to make it back to shore, but he and Mother Superior had an understanding. Rich honored and respected her and treasured her fish, and in return, she allowed him to travel on her unpredictable waves safely, even when she was angry and volatile. She reminded Rich several times over the years that she held the sole authority to break their understanding anytime she chose, but she always allowed him safe passage back to the land world from where he came.

The humming tapered off when Rich thought of that one time when she almost didn't honor their understanding. "Ahhh, that was stupid of me anyway," he scolded himself while reliving that terrifying experience for a moment.

Rich remembered paddling furiously up the Misery River in his canoe one April day several years ago when there were still ice banks on the sides of the river. The current was very strong with the high water level of the river from the melting snow. The electric trolling motor mounted on the left side of the canoe didn't have enough power to overcome the current and Rich paddled with all his strength to fight his way up the river to the launch area. Luckily, the marine battery powering the motor held out long enough for Rich to push the nose of the canoe onto the launch ramp. He remembered how exhausted he was afterwards and his whole body ached for days from paddling so hard to keep himself moving up the river.

But now, Rich had a three horsepower gas motor that he used to travel faster across Misery Bay and to also save the electric trolling motor for fishing. He also learned not to tempt Mother Superior's good graces by going out on her waters while there were still ice banks on her shores.

Rich pulled into the parking area near the Misery River and hopped out of the truck, noticing the slight waves on the lake with a light westerly breeze that wouldn't do much to slow his trek across Misery Bay to Wolf Point. Untying the canoe from the back of the truck and sliding it down the launch ramp, Rich felt the warmth of the sun on his back and removed his shirt, but not before sticking a fresh pinch of snuff in his lower lip. He tied one shirt sleeve to the cross brace nearest to the rear seat of the canoe for easy access to the snuff can in the shirt pocket.

Then he placed four heavy concrete bricks and two fifteen-pound mushroom anchors in the front of the canoe to balance out his weight from the back of the canoe. The electric trolling motor and marine battery went in the canoe next followed by two rods and the tackle box. A large net and a cooler were the last items inserted into the canoe before the five-gallon gas tank and gas motor took their place behind the backseat of the canoe.

Finally, the combination padded seat and flotation device was tossed on the rear seat as Rich pushed the front of the canoe into the river.

With his fishing vessel set for his journey, Rich pushed the canoe off from the launch ramp and hopped in as the slow current of the Misery River began pushing the canoe out to Lake Superior. He turned around to start the gas motor, and after two pulls, it came to life. Slowly steering the canoe out of the mouth of the Misery River, he gradually turned westward toward Wolf Point and accelerated the motor to cross the bay.

Rich looked forward into the distance and didn't see any boats on the horizon. There were no vehicles parked near the launch area, so he was guessing that he was alone to enjoy the near calm waters of Lake Superior. "What a beautiful day!" he said to himself, knowing that even he could barely hear his words over the chugging of the motor.

Nearly an hour had passed when Rich could finally see Wolf Point in the distance. As he came within a few hundred yards of Wolf Point, he shut off the motor and began setting up his rods, casting one lure to the left side and then casting another lure to the right side. Turning the handle of the electric motor, he began moving along toward the shoreline, letting out line on both rods until he turned the handle of each reel to lock the bail to bring the imitation minnow lures to life about 100 yards behind the canoe.

Within ten minutes, the right side rod began bouncing and Rich grabbed it from the rod holder and stopped the motor. He could tell that whatever was on the other end wasn't very big, but it had a pretty good fight to it. After reeling for about a minute, he could see that it was a small rainbow when he reeled it up to a few feet away from the canoe. Rich didn't have to even take it off the hook since the lure popped out of the rainbow's mouth as he began lifting it out of the water with the net. Smiling because he knew he wouldn't go home skunked, he put the net back into the water and allowed the fifteen-inch rainbow to swim away toward the bottom to let it grow for another year or two.

33. Vermilion Point Life Saving Station, one of five between
Grand Marais and White Fish Point, on Lake Superior.

Vermilion Life Saving Station

Casting the lure back out to the right side, Rich turned the electric motor to continue fishing. More than an hour passed with no more bites. Rich kept passing over the spots where he knew the fish were likely to be, but no luck. Another pass over the good spots and another hour went by. Five pinches of snuff over three hours and still nothing. "What the hell is going on?" Rich mumbled to himself, frustrated with the unlucky turning of the fishing tide.

A slight chill filled the air as Rich began to notice dark clouds several miles to the west. Frustrated, he said to himself, "Yeah, I guess it's time to pack up and start heading back." He reeled in the right side rod and stuck it on the bottom of the canoe.

Just then, the left side rod began bouncing forcefully and was nearly ripped out of the rod holder as Rich was about to pick it up and reel it in. As soon as Rich tugged on the rod, he knew that whatever was on the other end was no fifteen-inch rainbow. "Ha ha! Big Louie!" he yelled, using his favorite term for a big fish.

But Rich quickly realized that Big Louie wasn't going to give up the fight easily. Rich tried to reel the fish toward the canoe, but the drag on the reel wouldn't hold the line and Rich had to loosen the drag so the line wouldn't break. Big Louie wasn't going to get away after four hours of unproductive trolling, Rich swore to himself.

The chess match between Rich and Big Louie went on for twenty minutes with no clear winner to be determined. Rich felt his arms getting tired but he didn't want to lose whatever monster was on the other end. It never broke the surface so Rich didn't even know what he was battling.

Those dark clouds that were several miles away were now much closer and the wind became stronger and colder, pushing the canoe further from shore. Rich couldn't put the rod down to put on his shirt and he struggled to keep the canoe closer to the shoreline where he knew he could be within minutes if the lake became too rough. But he fought on, determined not to let Big Louie win the fight.

Another fifteen minutes and the clouds were almost directly over Rich. The wind pushed the canoe further out to the lake and the waves were beginning to toss the canoe around. Rich had no choice but to cut the line and let Big Louie go. He knew he only had minutes to get back to shore before the wind and waves would be too much for the canoe to handle.

Fumbling around in his tackle box to find the knife to cut the line, Rich looked up and saw several large waves coming toward the canoe. Yelling and swearing while finally locating the knife, he cut the line and threw the rod in the canoe and turned around to start the gas motor. One pull, two pulls, three pulls, four pulls, and then it finally started! Turning the accelerator handle all the way to the right, the motor revved up and began pushing the canoe toward the shore.

It was a valiant effort by Rich, but a huge wave pushed the canoe up over eight feet and slammed it back down. Then an even bigger wave elevated the canoe back up again before Rich lost sight of the bow as it turned back down almost vertically and disappeared into the water. Rich hung on to the sides of the canoe and plunged down into the water along with it before bobbing back up again, swallowing Lake Superior's cold water while gasping for breath.

Within seconds, another wave pushed the canoe up and flipped it end over end with nearly all of its contents instantly sinking to the bottom.

Wave after wave slammed the canoe down into the depths before the canoe bobbed back up again, destined to ride the waves like a ghost ship devoid of any passengers. It was on its own for the rest of the day and into the night, pummeled mercilessly by Mother Superior's waters, but not allowed to sink to her bottom along with its pilot and his belongings.

The next morning, Jonny was leaning against Rich's truck by the launch ramp when he heard a garbled voice from the crackling radio in the Coast Guard SUV parked next to him. The Coast Guard officer talked back into the radio and a frown came over his face as the voice that came back over the radio gave him the information he didn't want to hear.

Getting out of the SUV, the Coast Guard officer approached Jonny and said, "Our search and rescue team found your broth-er's canoe washed up on the shore by Wolf Point. The registration numbers on the canoe match with our marine craft registration records. It's Rich's canoe. But there's no sign of Rich anywhere. Maybe he made it back to shore and decided to walk to get some help."

Jonny's head fell downwards and his heart suddenly felt cold. He began to cry.

"He could still be out there. We'll keep looking for him." The Coast Guard officer said to Jonny.

Jonny nodded and asked, "Can you bring the canoe back here? I'll take it home in my truck. I'll leave Rich's truck here for now if he shows up."

"Yeah, I'll have them tow it back. I'm sorry, Jonny," he said, patting Jonny on the shoulder before turning back to the SUV to wait for the canoe to arrive.

After waiting for about an hour while looking out over Lake Superior and pondering if his brother was still alive, Jonny could see a boat cruising across Misery Bay. The Coast Guard boat slowed while entering the mouth of the Misery River. Jonny could see his brother's canoe tied to the side of the boat. Jonny walked back to the launch ramp to wait for the canoe so he could take it home.

The canoe was shoved onto the ramp by the Coast Guard officers and Jonny approached it with caution. He could see the large dents in the bottom and the sides where it must have hit some rocks.

And then he saw Rich's blue shirt still tied to the rear cross brace. Jonny began to weep as he bent down to touch the shirt. The can of snuff was still in the buttoned pocket.

"She took him fishing one last time...and now he's with her forever," Jonny sobbed.

Mother Superior got her catch that day.

Jan (Jon) Wisniewski lives in Gwinn with his wife Heather. Jan wrote this story in remembrance of his deceased brother, Ryszard "Roscoe" Wisniewski, who loved fishing on Lake Superior. Although Lake Superior didn't claim Roscoe's life, she did claim his heart and soul.

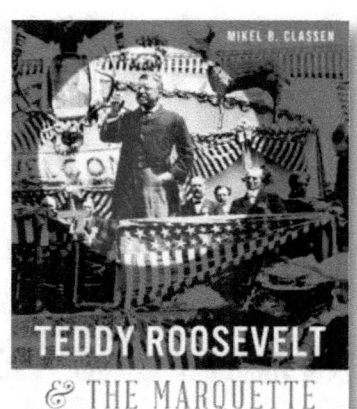

www.ingramcontent.com/pod-product-compliance
Lightning Source LLC
Chambersburg PA
CBHW080740250626
47170CB00010B/2894